ISBN 978-1-333-01389-9
PIBN 10450919

THE "HEAPED" FIRE

Readers of "The Studio" who desire to enhance the

Comfort and Distinction

of their rooms by the addition of notably tasteful and interesting

Furniture, Carpets, Curtains, &c.

— At the most competitive London prices —

are specially invited to write for HAMPTONS' Illustrated Catalogues,
which may be had post free, together with specially prepared
furnishing schemes, etc., on receipt of particulars
of the applicants' requirements.

Hampton's No. C 2056 6-ft. Sideboard in Mahogany, adapted by
Hamptons from an old Chippendale Model.

For many other Examples of Best Current Values in Dining
Room Furniture, see Catalogue No. C 329 sent post free.

HAMPTONS

Pall Mall East, Trafalgar Square, London, S.W.

AD. XII

OLD ENGLISH
COUNTRY COTTAGES

EDITED BY CHARLES HOLME

OFFICES OF ‚THE STUDIO,' LONDON
PARIS, AND NEW YORK   MCMVI

PREFATORY NOTE.

" Would it look well in a painting ? " is a test question which it has been recommended should be considered when the enquirer is in doubt as to the artistic value of some structural or ornamental object. A favourable answer is by no means an infallible guide to the principles of Art ; but the enquiry is, nevertheless, sufficiently useful to warrant it being made upon many occasions. When we consider it in relation to the rustic dwellings with which our English country landscape is dotted, we find the answer to be over-whelmingly in favour of those of ancient build. The modern ones with their yellow bricks, slate roofs, tarred weather boards and corrugated iron, are entirely opposed to all ideas of the beautiful. The ancient cottage harmonises with its surroundings, the modern one is at variance with them. The mere age of the former may add an element of beauty to it, but to the latter even the weathering of the years will have no very kindly influence. To preserve some record of these fast disappearing old buildings has been the object of the Editor in the preparation of this volume. He, how-ever, makes no claim to have exhausted the subject. To do so within the compass of a single volume, or, indeed, of many, would be impossible. But he trusts that the material which has here been accumulated may be of interest and service both to present and future students of the subject. He desires especially to record his thanks to Mrs. Lionel Beddington, Mrs. Bolton, Mr. R. L. Gunther, Mr. W. F. Unsworth, Mr. Herbert Alexander, A.R.W.S., Mr. Wilfrid Ball, R.E., Mr. E. A. Chadwick, Mrs. Stanhope Forbes, A.R.W.S., Mr. Wilmot Pilsbury, R.W.S., Mrs. M. Stormont and Mr. Grosvenor Thomas, for their kindly loan of the paintings reproduced in colours herein. Also to Sir Benjamin Stone, M.P., and Mr. T. A. Cossins, for the valuable assistance they rendered Mr. Sydney R. Jones in the preparation of his drawings which illustrate this volume, by placing at his disposal their wide knowledge of the subject.

ILLUSTRATIONS IN COLOUR

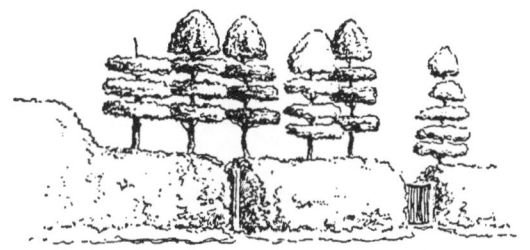

CONTENTS.

vii

INTRODUCTION

HOLLINGBOURNE, KENT. FROM A WATER-COLOUR DRAWING BY MRS. ALLINGHAM, R.W.S.
(By Permission of Mrs. Lionel Beddington.)

INTRODUCTION

*T*HERE is probably no object so much a natural part of the English landscape, nor which makes such a direct appeal to the heart and imagination, as the old country cottage. In every part of England, in the village and on the outskirts of the town, in the hamlet and standing on the lonely moor, there still remain those beautiful witnesses to the vitality, freshness, and pride of the village mason and carpenter. Passing from district to district the wonder grows at the many types, and that half a day's journey from cottages of stone there are cottages of cob and thatch. To understand fully the significance of these changes has to realise that England is divided into geological provinces, that their inhabitants have not always sprung from the same stock. Some parts came directly under the influence of the alien, and others under that of the towns, while those in remote parts developed in the

they were brought into contact with the village craftsman at first again probably during the building of the church, but nearly

travelling body of craftsmen, if there were such, may have given rise to the development of a district or particular locality, but the constant and abiding influence was that which came from the soil. The configuration of the land, the materials, the climate—these are constant. It were difficult to find a more striking illustration of inspiration the soil than in these cottages throughout England. Scholarship, and art, in the sense understood are seldom seen, and it is almost impossible to conceive of mason or carpenter regarding himself as an artist. Content to from generation to generation the traditions of the locality in which born, work varied little in expression, but much in degree; one with more imagination than his fellows gave a finished a gable with a finial of a fresh added another variety of walling; one carried through his a little in advance, and one remained a little behind, but the work whole was customary and usual, and the following on of what fathers had done before them. Each gave of his best, his quota simple and direct workmanship, using the materials that were to hand, sometimes wisely and well, sometimes badly, but always inspired with a fancy and invention as natural as they were unconscious. The way they built and the way we build are essentially different. With them the tendency was to add gradually new methods of doing things, slowly increasing their

HOLLINGBOURNE, KENT. FROM A WATER-COLOUR DRAWING BY H. ALLINGHAM, R.W.S.

INTRODUCTION

*T*HERE is probably no object so much a natural part of the English landscape, nor which makes such a direct appeal to the heart and imagination, as the old country cottage. In every part of England, in the village and on the outskirts of the town, in the hamlet and standing on the lonely moor, there still remain these beautiful witnesses to the vitality, freshness, and pride of the village mason and carpenter. Passing from district to district the wonder grows at the many types, and that half a day's journey from cottages of stone there are cottages of cob and thatch. To understand fully the significance of these changes one has to realise that England is divided into geological provinces, and that their inhabitants have not always sprung from the same stock. Some parts came directly under the influence of the alien, and others under that of the towns, while those in remote parts developed in the neighbourhood of the church and the manor.

The members of the town guilds were possibly another influence when they were brought into contact with the village craftsmen at fair time, and again probably during the building of the church ; but neither the towns nor the guilds, the church nor the alien, are sufficient to account for the individuality and charm of the country cottage. The appearance of a travelling body of craftsmen, if there were such, may have given an impetus to the development of a district or particular locality, but the real permanent and abiding influence was that which came from the soil. The configuration of the land, the materials, the climate—these are constant. It would be difficult to find a more striking illustration of inspiration through the soil than in these cottages throughout England. Scholarship, learning, and a knowledge of building and art, in the sense understood by us to-day, are seldom seen, and it is almost impossible to conceive of the local mason or carpenter regarding himself as an artist. Content to carry on from generation to generation the traditions of the locality in which they were born, work varied little in expression, but much in detail. The craftsman with more imagination than his fellows gave a new turn to the mouldings, finished a gable with a finial of a fresh pattern, or added another variety of walling ; one carried through his work a little in advance, and one remained a little behind, but the work as a whole was customary and usual, and the following on of what their fathers had done before them. Each gave of his best, his quota of simple and direct workmanship, using the materials that were to hand, sometimes wisely and well, sometimes badly, but always inspired with a fancy and invention as natural as they were unconscious. The way they built and the way we build are essentially different. With them the tendency was to add gradually new methods of doing things, slowly increasing their store of ideas, from which they drew, as they drew water from the well on the village green. The source of inspiration for all of them was the same. With us the tendency is to reduce the many ways to as few as possible, and in the place of local materials to substitute a manufactured one that can be applied universally. If an inventive genius like Mr. Barrie's sentimental Tommy "finds a way" to place upon the markets of the world a material that fulfils the function of a wall, roof, floor, and foundation, indeed all that is generally required in a modern cottage, he will earn the gratitude of those well-meaning philanthropists who want "cheap" cottages. The links are broken in the old building traditions of the country side, not merely through the exodus of the rural population and the change in social conditions, but by the almost complete abandonment of the old conceptions of life and work. The cottages of the past were built for use by the villager, whereas the new are built for cheapness and profit or by philanthropists, a distinction perhaps without a great difference. To build once more in the same spirit must mean a return to their traditions, the reopening of local quarries, the revival and encouragement of local industries, methods of work, pride in craftsmanship and the total abolition of "cheapness" as a standard for approval. And this will come to pass just as surely as the day follows the night and spring the winter, and in due season will blossom work as beautiful as that done by the men who laid stone to stone on the Cotswold Hills, or of those who thatched the barns and hayricks of Norfolk and Suffolk. No aspect of English building is so full of surprises as the study of countryside architecture. One village is mediæval and another classic in spirit, while again others have the characteristics of both. At one side of a county are cottages of brick, at the other, of stone ; galleting in Kent differs from galleting in Surrey. Brick walls are as varied in bond as the courses of the masonry. Neatness, order, and well-kept hedges and gardens in one district, the reverse in the next. These expressions, local and particular, noticeable everywhere, have given to our villages their individual stamp. A natural conservatism and narrowness of outlook, an absence of easy means of communication between districts lying apart, have helped to foster and encourage the local methods of work. Alterations and new fashions in detail came so slowly, and fresh methods of building once perhaps during a generation, that even in the districts where it is possible to trace the foreign influence, the native workmen have moulded afresh the ideas of the foreigner, adding local character in the course of transmutation. In the treatment of surfaces the villager was a master. " What," says the late J. D. Sedding, " was roughish, tool-marked freestone in the old building, is smooth, machine-dressed bath-stone in the new. What was built of many-tinted, thin, uneven-shaped bricks in the old place, is built of regular shaped and of hard, monotonous colour in the new ; what was of coarse plaster in the old, is smooth, speckless stucco in the new. What was rough-burnt tile or hand-shaped timber, or hand-cast plaster, or hand-wrought iron in the old, is machine-made, dead, textureless in the new." The use of contrasting materials was common, sometimes deliberately adopted, and sometimes, we suspect, owing to a limited supply of a material. Comparatively smooth stone was introduced into rough brick, flint intermingled with brick, stones projected from wall faces, joints were galleted and geometrical patterns were stamped in plaster, and the simpler device of leaving the trowel marks or dotting with marks, not unlike those made by the gouge in woodwork, were among the methods used by the plasterer. There are cottages between districts which have methods common to both, tile-hung dwellings with stone slates and rough-cast walls jostling those of stone.

In the arrangement of materials, whether of one or of many, the village workman displayed a happy knack of doing the right thing in the right place, but in putting them together he was not always so successful, and seldom satisfactory from the sanitary expert's point of view. The rain was allowed to drop from the eaves without any means to collect it, the water to sink into the foundations, and walls were sometimes badly built ; but in spite of these drawbacks, and possibly partly owing to them, the appeal of the country cottage is universal. To the painter they are a subject for the brush ; to the pen-and-ink artist, a study in black and white ; and to the architect, a temptation to crib. The old cottage appears to have always exercised an uncanny power over the mind of the painter, for there is a singular unanimity amongst them to paint it in a state of collapse, with pigs in the foreground, a ragged cottager at the door, and sometimes a ladder leaning against it, like a flying buttress, as if the painter felt that without this support it would never stand up at all. Nor is it only to the professional person that they appeal. The saying, "Love in a cottage," still has its significance for all simple and homely people, and in the last generation our fathers and mothers regarded the cottage as the ideal home ; the drawing-books of their children were not thought complete without an example of "The Country Cottage" set before them as the crowning achievement and completion of their education with pencil and pen.

The plan seems to have had an origin quite distinct from that of the circular hut. At first it was merely a copy of the simple rectangular structures erected for the housing of the oxen. It was built in bays to accommodate what was called a long yoke of oxen, that is four abreast, and the bays divided by two pairs of bent trees, in form resembling the lancet-shaped arches of a Gothic church, and placed at 16-feet intervals. These were set upon the ground, united at their apex by a ridge tree, and the framework strengthened by two tie-beams and four wind braces, and fastened together by wooden pegs. The couples or trusses were usually known as "forks," and curved for the object of giving more head room.[1] There is a cottage at Crudgington, in Shropshire, in which the main timbers follow the principle of this construction. The angle posts at the corners of the gable ends spring from the ground and curve more or less towards the ridge, and at the eaves' level the timbers correspond to the cross-piece in the construction of the old barn ; the rest of the timbering fills in the space between in the usual way. During the first stages of cottage building this was undoubtedly the architectural unit, the length of

[1] "Evolution of the English House," by Sidney O. Addy, M.A.

the dwelling determined by the number of bays or half bays and the rooms required. In a later development it was increased in width by the addition of outshoots at the side, like the transept of a church, much in the same manner that the outhouses are tacked on to a modern dwelling. In this simple fashion developed the plan of the ancient cottage, any variations of it arising from some special requirements. Although this plan persisted for so many generations, modifications crept in owing to the nature of the materials. The cob walls of a Somersetshire or Devonshire cottage were nearly always built with rounded angles, and in instances which have come directly under the observation of the writer, cottages at the corners of two roads were planned to follow semi-circular lines. Of this influence of material upon the form the general appearance of the cottages in other districts afford examples. For instance, when stone slabs of a large size were used for covering the roof, the pitch was flat, as at Horsham and the surrounding neighbourhood, and in other parts the pitch of the roof for tiles was something between thatch and the heavy stone roofs. Returning once more to the plan, a comparison of districts tends to show that originally all were based on the same simple parallelogram, with or without outshoots on one side, or by the addition of other bays when more accommodation was required. In some cases the cottages were only one bay, that is sixteen feet, with perhaps an outshoot on one side and the oven projecting beyond. In a Surrey cottage showing additions to the old portion, the original structure measures exactly sixteen feet, but in the new part the principle of the " bay " was not observed. Occasionally the additions were made on the long side, and the roof continued down over the new part. As long as the cottage was built with " forks " as couples and wattle and daub as filling-in, it was not unreasonable to expect a more or less close adherence to the architectural unit ; but it appears to have been followed when the construction was of stone. Many of the Cotswold plans are either multiples of the " bay " (sixteen feet) or the " half bay " (eight feet). This may be a coincidence, but the survival in one material of the old method formerly used in another has often been noticed by writers on architecture. The width of the cottages in both Surrey and Gloucestershire was generally from sixteen to eighteen feet. Another example of the influence of material upon planning is the position of the fireplace and oven. In cottages of wood construction and plaster filling-in they were nearly always kept on the outside walls, and were of great bulk, while in the stone examples this was only done to a limited extent, the fireplace in many instances, probably the majority, being built inside the main structure. Wherever the fireplace is placed on the cross walls, the stairs almost invariably adjoin it, the limited space necessitating winders both at the beginning and the end. The fireplace and chimney-stack were often preserved when all else had been pulled down. In Kent, for instance, chimney stacks are frequently built in English bond, the rest having been rebuilt in Flemish. As a general rule in the early cottages the bricks are laid English bond, while Flemish is adopted in those of a later date. Although the plan remains much the same all over England, except for such relatively unimportant points as have been noted, the difference in the

6

types of buildings is remarkable. A comparison of a Cotswold and a Somersetshire cottage shows how the material has affected the result. Nor is there so much variety, skill, and thought in the Southern as in the Northern examples. The neatness and order found in Gloucestershire, and the care in thatching, are missing in the Somersetshire and Devonshire cottages. There is a want of tidiness in the methods of the latter. A hard-and-fast classification of these types is unnecessary—and, indeed, would be difficult to arrange satisfactorily—but certain counties may be grouped and localised by the materials commonly used in the neighbourhood. In Suffolk and Norfolk flint and brick walls and pantiles are the chief materials for cottages, while the long barns characteristic of this part are of tarred weatherboarding, with wonderful steep-pitched thatched roofs. Somersetshire and Devonshire build cob and slatey stone walls, plastered and whitewashed, and roofed with thatch. Half-timber and brick, brick and plaster walls, with tiles and thatched roofs, were general in Warwickshire and Worcestershire ; and in Kent, Sussex, and Surrey brick and timber, plaster, weatherboarding and weather-tiling were used for the walls, and tiles for the roofs. Gloucestershire and Oxfordshire depended chiefly on stone ; and Cheshire, Shropshire, and Herefordshire, like the Midland counties, used half-timber and brick, and brick and plaster for the walls, and stone slates for the roofs in Cheshire, and tiles in the other two counties. Derbyshire used stone, like the Cotswold district.

Some of the most interesting villages are more or less characteristic of two districts. Mickleton, in Gloucestershire, although some little distance south, after the Warwickshire border has been crossed, supplies an instance of this mingling of two types. There are cottages of whitewashed brick, that have thatched roofs, walls of rough-cast with stone slate roofs and dormers, arranged like those in Warwickshire ; cottages of brick and timber, the brick whitewashed, and the whole erected on a stone base covered with stone slate roofs, and others of brick and timber with thatched roofs. The mixture of brick and stone is common. The workmanship in the masonry is as careful, and the reverse, as in more typical Gloucestershire villages ; in some cases it is coursed and in others partly coursed and partly irregular. In the same village there are the characteristic stepped brick verges usual in Warwickshire and Worcestershire. Ebrington, two or three miles to the east of Chipping Campden, in the district of stone walls, mullioned windows, and stone slates, is a village of cottages built of stone walls, very few mullioned windows, with roofs of thatch, a few only being of stone. While Mickleton is well within the borders of Gloucestershire, and Ebrington is close to the finest examples of stone cottages, Broadway, in Worcestershire, is almost entirely characteristic of the Gloucestershire type. At Welford-on-Avon, in Gloucestershire, and close to the boundaries of Warwickshire, the cottages are more characteristic of the last-named county. They have the same frieze-like scheme of walling over the ground-floor windows, obtained by the sills of the dormers ranging with the eaves. This is a strongly-marked feature of Warwickshire, and it is also found in the borderland cottages, while the tradition survives in stone in some of the Cotswold villages.

KENT, SUSSEX, SURREY, HAMPSHIRE

CRANBROOK, KENT. FROM A WATER-COLOUR DRAWING BY HERBERT ALEXANDER, A.R.W.S.

DIVISION I

KENT, SUSSEX, SURREY, HAMPSHIRE

I.—KENT, SUSSEX, SURREY, AND HAMPSHIRE

ENT, Sussex, and Surrey are three of the most delightful counties in England, and three of the richest in cottages that depend for their distinctive character upon the effective use of three, four, and even five materials. A certain number of them are on somewhat similar lines to those in Shropshire and Herefordshire; but it is proposed here to consider more especially the examples of brick and timber, weatherboarding, tile-hanging, and tile roofs in West Kent and Surrey; those roofed with stone at Horsham and the surrounding neighbourhood; those of stone roofed with thatch, found in Sussex; those of flint and stone roofed with tile, to the east of Kent; and some of those in Hampshire with tile-hanging and tile roofs. Roughly and briefly, the general character of the early ones is mediæval both in construction and feeling, while that of those later in date is classic in spirit, retaining much the same method of construction and workmanship. This classic —or, to be more accurate, Georgian— spirit which pervades so many of them asserts itself in the proportions, the unbroken eaves, the absence of dormers, and the subordination of the gables that generally break out of the roof at a low level, leaving the main roof uninterrupted between the

TONBRIDGE, KENT

11

large chimneys flanking the gable ends, or divided by one large stack in the middle. At Hollingbourne (see frontispiece) and at Witley (opposite page 38) is seen this horizontal character, and also in the cottage at Penshurst (page 20) and those in the foreground of the drawing of Goudhurst (page 17). A comparison of the roof coverings in these counties with those of the Cotswold district shows what great differences may arise in the use of two dissimilar materials. In the Cotswold we have narrow spans, steep stone-slated roofs, with an almost universal gable treatment; in the above counties wider spans and a general tendency, particularly in later work, to lower-pitched roofs, hipped at both ends. The only district where stone-slated roofs were hipped was in the heart of the tile counties. Here there are a number, the builders merely following the tradition of tile-roofing. In one example near Crawley, North Sussex, (page 35), and in another just over the border, at Chiddingfold, Surrey (page 37), the hipped ends have the same little gablets that occur in so many of the Surrey cottages, and less often in Kent and Hampshire. These grew out of the manner of constructing the hipped ends. As no ridge-board was used, " it was therefore obviously inconvenient to run the hip-rafters together to a point, and they were therefore run each to about nine inches below the junction of the pair of rafters. This of course caused the little gablet,"[1] and gave a piquant effect to the ends, as seen in the drawings

[1] "Old Cottage and Domestic Architecture, South-West Surrey," Ralph Nevill, F.S.A., F.R.I.B.A.

BIDDENDEN, KENT

CRANBROOK, KENT

13

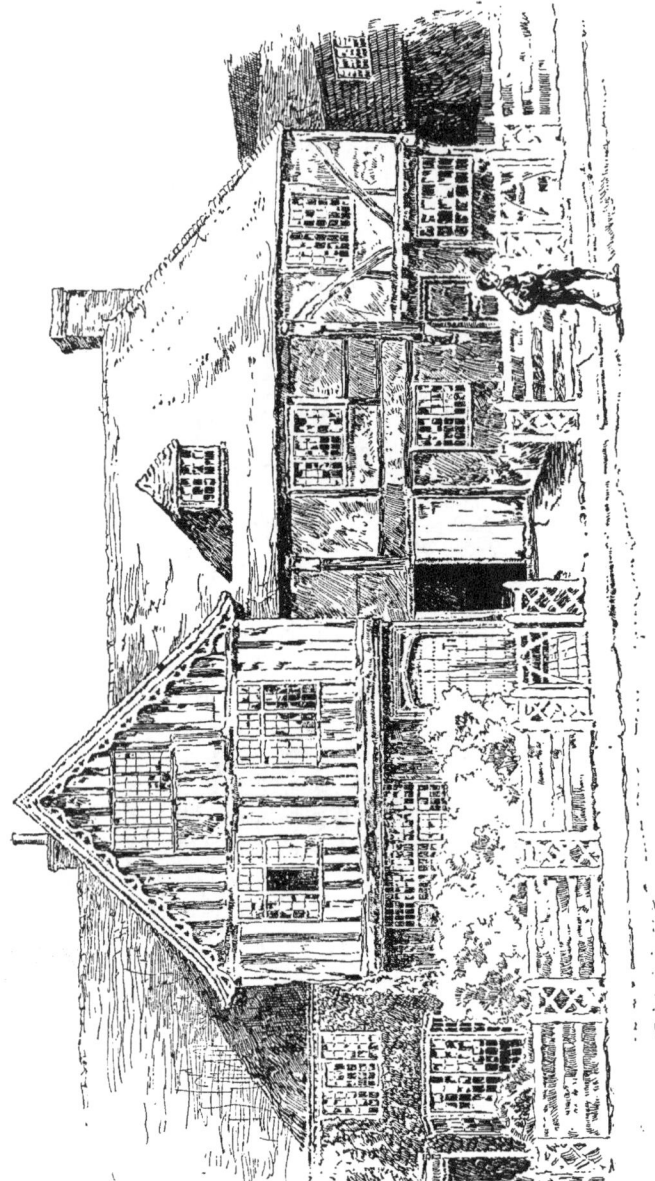

CRANBROOK, KENT

facing page 40. It is worth noticing, as an illustration of the conservatism of these cottage builders and their tenacity in keeping to the old ways, that the form of roof adopted to take the chief roofing material of a district was followed when a sudden change in the geological formation of the county compelled them to use another. For instance, when heavy stone slabs were used for the roof in the middle of a tile district the hipped ends were retained, although the pitch of the roof was made flatter, as in the cottage illustrated on page 35. Or, again, if thatch was used in Sussex, the tile roof of hipped form still persisted (see drawing on page 31) ; and in the Cotswold district, if thatch took the place of stone slates, the roofs were gabled, as in the cottage

UPPER DEAL, KENT

CANTERBURY, KENT

illustrated on page 85 ; even the stone-coped gables were retained in some cases with the thatched roof.

There is a rather picturesque method of treating the walls in Surrey. Small pieces of ironstone are inserted in the joints of the brickwork; if a stone wall and the blocks do not hold up to the corners, these are also filled in as well as the joints : this forms a kind of mosaic and gives colour and variety to the wall. In Kent another method is adopted for the coursed rag masonry ; in this case small pieces of flint are placed in the joints close together and in a sloping direction, giving an effect like a conventional rope pattern. The use of brick in these counties varies considerably. The chimneys of the cottage at Penshurst, in Kent (page 21), show two or three methods. For instance, the set-offs of the buttresses are obtained by laying the bricks at right angles to the slopes, and just under the base they are laid on the flat. This chimney, flanking the side wall of the cottage, with the lower part of stone and brick, and above the base all in brick, is a charming example of a well-proportioned Kent chimney. The whole cottage shows an exceptional and effective use of brick and timber, plaster and tiles and weather-boarding in the gable end. These chimney shafts throughout this county are of extraordinary beauty and proportions. Every village, one might say almost every cottage, shows some individuality, either in the plan of the fines or in the oversailing of the brick caps ; and yet withal it is impossible to mistake a Kent chimney for one of any other district. Near Newenden (page 25), the panels are plastered between the end pilasters; and occasionally the contrast between the plaster and brick is reversed, the piers being plastered and the panels of brick. The cap is formed by two slightly projecting courses of brick, one beyond the other, two more courses above to form another set-off, and a necking two or three courses below. At Petworth, in Sussex (page 25), the long sides are broken by the projecting withes of brickwork that probably divide the flue, and the cornice is carried round it, formed, in the way already described, by courses of brick. Byworth, in Sussex (page 25), is another interesting example, much the same, only with two projecting withes close together, and the top courses forming the cap of another profile. At Northiam, to the east of

GOUDHURST, KENT

16

GOUDHURST, KENT

18

Sussex and on the borders of Kent (page 25), the plan of the stack is again somewhat different, the cornice is without necking and the arrangement of the set-offs changed. A rather unusual type occurs at Sandhurst Green (page 25), in Kent; four octagon-shaped shafts rise from a square base with a space between each. Most of them rise out of the roof without any base except for the projecting course, forming a kind of drip above the tiles. The width of these chimneys does not alter very much, the great majority being 1 foot 10½ inches, that is two-and-a-half bricks, and occasionally three bricks wide.

It has already been pointed out that the brickwork in the earlier cottages is of English bond, and of Flemish in the later examples. The number of courses in a given height is also different, the former taking five courses to eleven-and-a-half inches, and the latter four or thereabouts; the joints, too, in English bond are wider; and in Flemish bond flared headers are almost invariably used. Another method of bricklaying is to place the bricks on end, with stretchers also placed on end, but

Angley

Canterbury

Canterbury

WOOD BRACKETS IN KENT

parallel instead of at right angles to the wall face, the courses then being 4½ inches deep instead of 2¼ inches. Between half-timber work they are laid in courses or stretchers or herring-bone fashion. In other walls the bricks are occasionally laid one header to three stretchers, and in Sussex, in the stone district, bands of stone are

WINDOW IN WOOD AND PLASTER
CANTERBURY, KENT

19

sometimes introduced in brick walls of English bond.   Brick dentil
courses, the dentil the width of a header, are common in Sussex, under
the tile-hanging of the first floor, and dentils the width of a small closer,
with the same space between, were noticed at Chiddingfold, Surrey.
The cottage near Crawley, in Sussex (page 35), close to the borders of
Surrey, is a typical example of the curious mixture of stone-slate roofs, tile-
hung first storey, with timber and brick on the ground floor.   Hipped at
one end like a tile roof and gabled on the return, which juts out at the further
side in a picturesque fashion, it illustrates one of those rare examples of
ornamental and plain tiling used successfully.   The iron stays supporting
the gutter are brought in most effectively.   Altogether, this is a charming
cottage, charmingly drawn.   At Goudhurst, probably the most beautiful
village in Kent (pages 16 and 17), some of the cottages have a distinctly
Georgian feeling, while others are of an earlier type.   In the foreground
of the larger drawing the open wooden loggia on the right shows a favourite
way of treating a shop.   In the middle distance are examples of weather-
boarded cottages ;   and up the street, at the far end, tile-hung fronts.
Another characteristic village is Cranbrook (page 13), and the cottage
(page 14) shows a combination of wood and brick and wood and plaster,
with pierced and carved barge boards on the overhanging gable ends ;   in
the later examples these are often placed directly on the wall face, as at
Wilsley House (opposite page 9), a good type of the half-timber dwellings
in and around this village.   Most of the early cottages are of timber
framing and plaster.   The timber, in nearly every case, is of oak, and

PENSHURST, KENT

PENSHURST, KENT

21

22

PENSHURST, KENT

" the panel is formed by fixing upright hazel rods in grooves cut in top and bottom, and by then twisting thinner hazel wands hurdlewise round them. The panel is then filled up solid with a plaster of marly clay and chopped straw, and finished with a thin coat of lime plaster."[1]

One of the features of the Surrey cottage, indeed of all those counties where tile was the principal roofing material, is the skill with which the tiling is adapted to its purpose. It covers the slopes of the buttresses and the gathering in of the big chimneys; it covers the roof and first-floor walls, works round the valleys and hips, and while never attaining to the freedom of Continental work of the same kind, suggests the possibilities of further development in its use. This art of covering surfaces with tiles was thoroughly understood by these cottage builders. They also used tiles in the cornices of the chimneys, introduced them into stone walling to make good, and sometimes covered their brick copings. The cottages at Witley (page 38) and those at the entrance to Guildford Castle (page 37), both in Surrey, show the usual use of this material, the first-floor storey of the gable end in the example at Witley projecting over the bay on the ground floor. In the tile-hanging, the lifting forward of the lower courses was assisted by projecting a course of brick about an inch-and-a-half, the edge of the lowest and double course covering part of the brickwork that jutted out.

At Goudhurst this outward curve is exaggerated into a hood extending the whole length of a row of cottages, projecting two feet from the wall faces and supported by wood brackets placed at regular intervals to take the plate and ends of the tiling. At Haslemere, in Surrey, the soffit of a similar arrangement takes the form of

SANDWICH, KENT

[1] " Old Cottage and Domestic Architecture, S.-W. Surrey," R. Nevill, F.S.A., F.R.I.B.A.

23

SANDWICH, KENT

24

a cove, the tiling being very cunningly hipped at the ends and joined up with the lean-to roof. At Tuesley, in Surrey, the same thing occurs without the plaster cove, the brackets jutting out like struts. Cottages where weather-boarding takes the place of tile-hanging, or hides the timbers and plaster of older fronts, are often covered with it entirely, with the exception of the base. When the lower edge of the boarding is left square, about five inches show with three-quarters of an inch projection beyond the one below. It is stopped at each end by small strips the whole height of the building, the narrow width facing outwards. The finish at the brick base or at the first-floor level is flat, and not tilted outwards as in tile-hanging. Sometimes the boarding has an ovolo on the bottom edge ; the vertical joints are over one another in many cases, but generally come in the most haphazard fashion. In the timber and brick and timber and plaster fronts, the sizes of the timbers do not appear to keep to any particular scantling, the intermediate and the horizontal pieces often being of comparatively small dimensions

Near Newenden

Petworth

Byworth

Sandhurst Green

Northiam

and varying from $4\frac{1}{2}$ ins. to 6 ins., and when less it appears as if the carpenter had deliberately placed them on the flat, with the narrow width of the timber exposed. The corner posts are from 9 ins. to 12 ins., and the braces larger. In one instance a careful afterthought was noticed. On the first floor the curved braces springing from the cill beam to the outside parts were tenoned and pinned direct into the upright, while on the floor above a splayed piece or thickening out near the top of the corner post was introduced to give an additional thickness and strength where it received the curved brace.

Another use of tile, particularly noticeable in parts of Surrey and

SANDWICH, KENT

Kent, is found in the copings and cornices of brick, where a fillet of one or two tiles is introduced to form a member. An instance of this occurs at Wingham in Kent, at Godalming and Farnham in Surrey, and at Sandwich in Kent (pages 23 and 24). In this last county generally there are some interesting examples of brick and stone treatment. Evidently inspired by Dutch methods, they yet show an unmistakable English character in their direct and simple construction and good decorative effects. The fronts of the buildings are panelled out in brick, and the panels formed by the projecting strips or pilasters of the same material. These projections vary from 1 in. to $1\frac{1}{2}$ in., and in some cases $2\frac{1}{2}$ ins. Simple geometrical patterns, such as squares and circles, connected by strips with bands above and below, toothed strips, and dressings of brickwork to the windows projecting in the same way, diamond and elliptical shapes raised on brick courses, and brick corbel courses, are all characteristics of this work. In the cornices of a few of the chimneys a member is sometimes formed of two or three bricks in depth. Another simple way of using brick is on the coped gables. A course of brick is carried beyond the face of the wall below, then come two bricks leaning towards each other, these being finished with others laid longways on. In Surrey and Kent the mediæval spirit continues more in construction than in the general form. The feeling for horizontal lines is noticed, for the cornice running from end to end of the unbroken eaves of even the simplest work soon became dominant after the early decades of the

LITTLE DIXTER, NORTHIAM, SUSSEX

Renaissance. Hawkhurst, in Kent, and the Cockshot cottages between the same village and Highgate, in Kent, both illustrate this tendency; and frequently in these cases where gables occur, the horizontal feeling is retained by the line and shadow caused by the projection of the gable beyond the face of the work beneath. Probably one of the reasons for the classic character of these cottages was due to their being near London and the larger towns that came more directly under the influence of the Renaissance revival. It is possible that the examples, and they are many, which have projecting wings at either end and a recessed hall, are a development of the classic tradition. It is a usual form with the old farm-houses in these districts. There is one at Compton, in Surrey, and at Goudhurst, in Kent. In Surrey it is tile-hung, and in Kent timber and plaster are used on the ground and first floors. In the details of the woodwork and in some of the metal fittings there is a curious mingling of classic detail with mediæval peculiarities of construction and methods of working. The doorway at the Post Office, Wickhambreaux, is constructed on mediæval principles, the jambs are chamfered, and the mouldings cut out of the solid; but, instead of stopping on a splayed rail, they return all round the panel.

BYWORTH, SUSSEX

28

BYWORTH, SUSSEX

29

The scroll-work too in the tympanum is of Classic character. Or take again the barge board at Wingham, Kent; it is essentially Gothic in its pierced work, but the moulding under the tiles has a hint of Classic feeling; and so also has the window head of the bay windows at Canterbury (pages 15 and 19). In the stairs at Stonehurst, Surrey, there is also this combination of Classic mouldings with Gothic construction and ornament.

FITTLEWORTH, SUSSEX

The mouldings of the newels and balusters are classic, while the construction of the staircase is mediæval as well as the powdering of the surface with stamps of varying forms. A characteristic of these old timber and plaster cottages is the plastering being flush with the timber.

The metalwork in these counties is of exceptionally fine character, and most of it is simply the shaping of the material into forms suitable for the purpose they have to fulfil; so, one might say, is the iron saucepan and the metal teapot produced to-day; but the early work happens to be both simple and beautiful, whereas the later is merely simple, commonplace and vulgar. Take any one of the objects of metalwork of the interior at Weston-Patrick, in Hampshire (page 43). The copper pot with its iron handle, the wooden coffee mill, the copper saucepan or the simple fire-dogs—every one is beautifully shaped, with special attention given to the purpose for which it is intended, and the demands of necessity and construction; such as the method of relieving the strain on the handle of the copper saucepan where it joins the side of the pan, or the

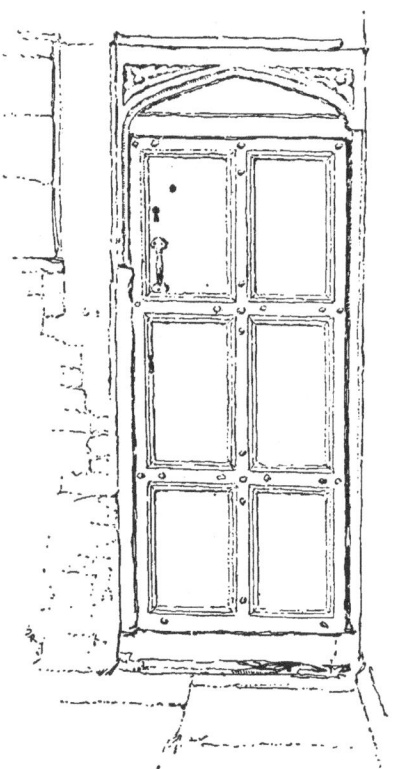

RYE, SUSSEX

30

FITTLEWORTH, SUSSEX

31

dainty scroll at the end of the semi-circular handle that hooks through the eye attached to the copper pot, the shaping of the feet of the fire-dog, or again the single shaped rod of the interior (page 42), on which the curtain is drawn. Another interior of a cottage near Northiam, in Sussex (page 34), shows the ingle from the inside of the hearth. It gives a good general notion of its ample dimensions, with the oven doors and the corbelling over of the flue ; the arched flying buttress in wood was evidently introduced to reduce the strain on the corbelling, an arrangement arising out of the old canopy of wood and plaster framework resting upon the chamber floor, and probably the origin of the stone chimney pieces of the large manor-houses. There is a large oak beam spanning the opening, a raised hearth in the middle, and a fireback.

Round about Maldon, and other parts of Essex, and indeed in many quite out-of-the-way districts, it is surprising how much really beautiful and refined detail there is to be found in the doors, windows and circular bow-windows of the village shops. Over and over again it strikes one what remarkably able craftsmen there were in these villages up to quite recent years, for the work is very late, and has often an Adams feeling in it, although in no way as elaborate in character. Pents with dainty and simple strap work on the soffits of wood, delicate reeding, and wonderfully refined contours to mouldings and modillions are commonplaces, and must have been executed long after the introduction of machinery for building purposes. Surrey and also Kent are full of this work. In Devonshire and Staffordshire, districts as far apart as these, is seen this type of refined and elegant detail, difficult to associate with the village and small town. It is similar in character to many of the old shop fronts still existing in different parts of London, and to the entrance doors of the houses in the squares about Bloomsbury.

PETWORTH, SUSSEX

32

PETWORTH, SUSSEX

33

NORTHIAM, SUSSEX

34

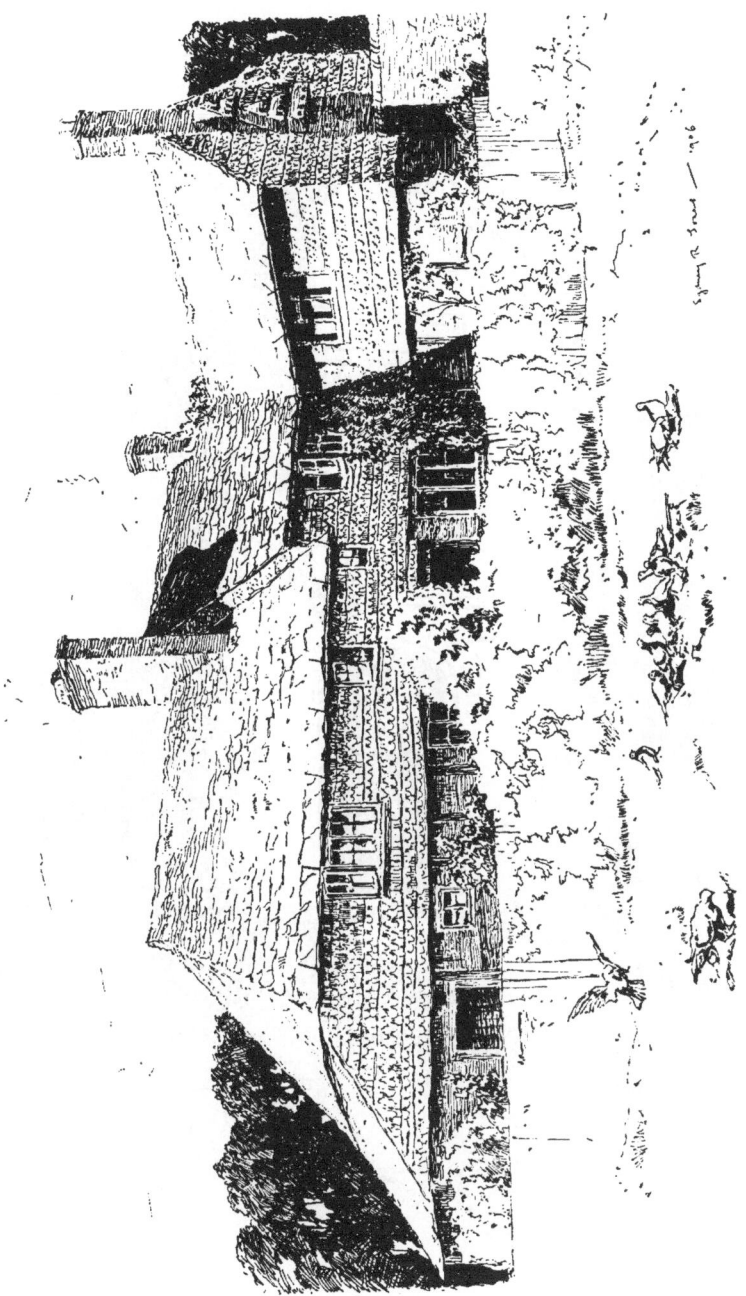

NORTH CHAPEL, SUSSEX

36

HASLEMERE, SURREY. FROM A WATER-COLOUR DRAWING BY MRS. ALLINGHAM, R.W.S.

CHIDDINGFOLD, SURREY

GUILDFORD CASTLE, SURREY

37

WITLEY, SURREY

WITLEY, SURREY

WITLEY, SURREY. FROM A WATER-COLOUR DRAWING BY MRS. M. STORMONT.

UPTON GREY, HAMPSHIRE

39

STEEP, HAMPSHIRE. FROM A WATER-COLOUR DRAWING BY WALTER TYNDALE.

(By Permission of W. F. Unsworth, Esq.)

Restoration from
old cottage at Steep
Petersfield –
W.F.Unsworth Archt –

STEEP, HAMPSHIRE. FROM A WATER-COLOUR DRAWING BY WALTER TYNDALE.

(By Permission of W. F. Unsworth, Esq.)

GREYWELL, HAMPSHIRE

· GREYWELL, HAMPSHIRE

Sydney R Jones — 1906

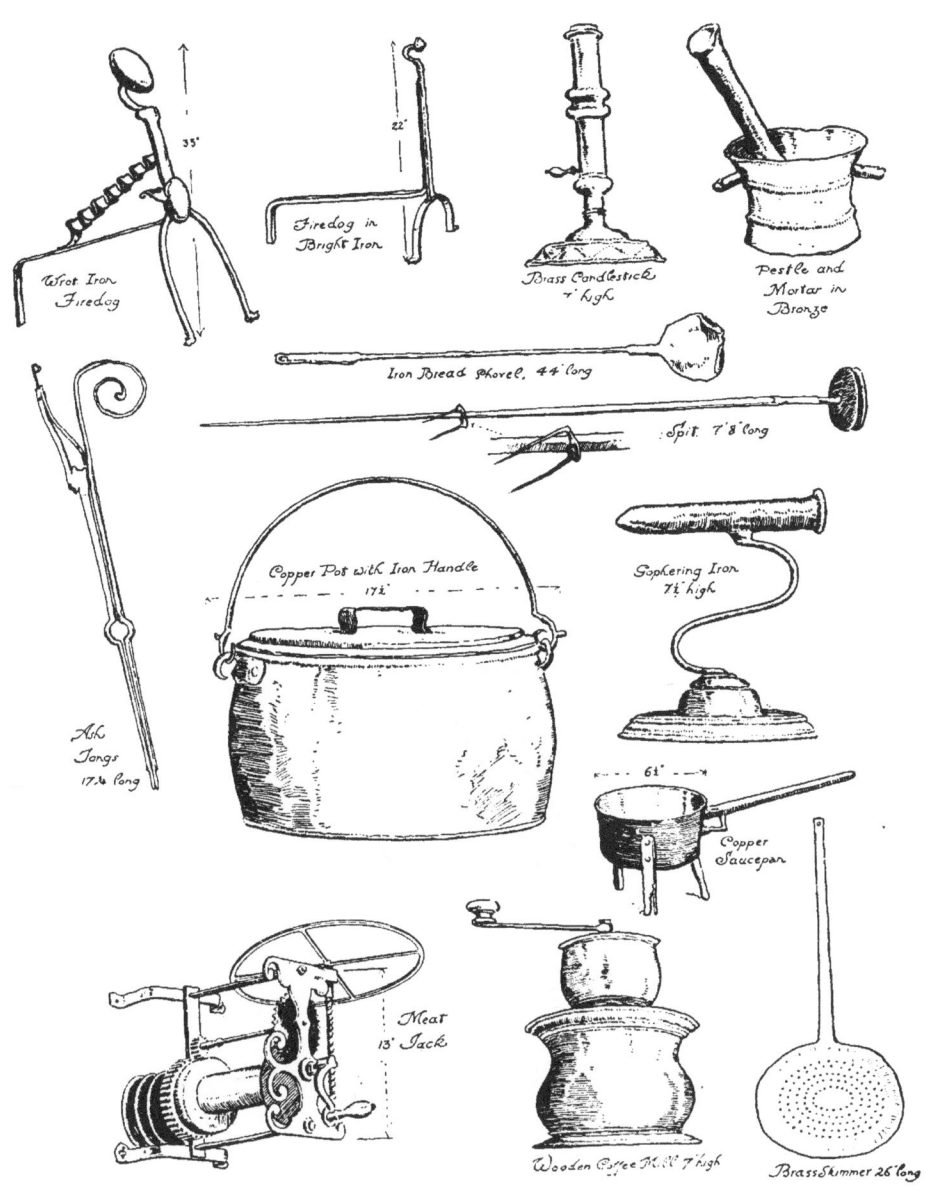

Wrot. Iron Firedog

Firedog in Bright Iron

Brass Candlestick 7' high

Pestle and Mortar in Bronze

Iron Bread Shovel, 44' long

Spit 7'8' long

Ash Tongs 17¾ long

Copper Pot with Iron Handle 17½'

Spokering Iron 7½ high

Copper Saucepan

Meat 13' Jack

Wooden Coffee Mill 7'high

Brass Skimmer 26' long

DETAILS OF FIREPLACE ACCESSORIES AT WESTON-PATRICK, HAMPSHIRE

DIVISION II.

SUFFOLK AND NORFOLK

II.—SUFFOLK AND NORFOLK

"HE re-introduction of brickwork in England," says Mr. Reginald Blomfield, "was probably due to two causes—first, to the scarcity of building stones in the neighbourhood, and secondly to the large immigration of Flemings into the Eastern Counties." It is therefore singular that so few examples of cottages on the east coast of Suffolk and Norfolk show the same wonderful skill in the use of brick as in Kent. The larger houses, some of the smaller ones, and occasionally the buildings in the towns, are treated in the fanciful, picturesque and masterly way common in the Netherlands. At Yarmouth, the rows (pages 56 and 57), and a street in Sandwich (page 24), possess a distinctly foreign character. The steep mansard-shaped gable at the end of the lane on the left (page 57), the cobble paving and narrow width of flagging down the middle, the open gutters next the walls, are all suggestive of an alien influence. But the villages and the country districts apparently were only influenced indirectly, owing probably to the natural tendency of the foreigner to prefer the large towns, and even there he does not seem to have actually engaged in building. From the lists of the artizans who settled in the towns on the east coast, it is seen that only a small number of foreigners were actually connected with the building trades. At Sandwich, in East Kent, three joiners, one carpenter, and one smith are mentioned. The natural inference is that the foreigner was more responsible for peculiarities than essentials; and this is so, for in spite of

WESTON, SUFFOLK

47

a foreign flavour about both the cottages and the scenery, the principal characteristics are those common to English work. There is the same simple, direct and intimate way of treating materials, added to a love of quaint conceits and a more fanciful but less workmanlike notion in the use of them. There is a playfulness too in the methods of using brick and flint, and in some of the gables, simplified treatments of the extravagant and fantastic curves loved by the Dutchmen. But these are few and far between ; the majority of cottage gables are almost as English in feeling as the stone buildings of Gloucestershire. At Weston, in Suffolk (page 49), the Dutch influence is noticeable in the brick quoins (page 164), the rounding of the gable at the apex, and in the filling of the tympanum of the arches over the doors (page 47), windows, and again in the dentils under the soffits. The finish of the four-and-a-half brick arches, which slightly project from the face of the main wall (page 164), is much the same method adopted at the intersection of the contrasting curves in the cottage at Yarmouth (page 55). Notwithstanding these suggestions of foreign detail, there is an English character about the build-

ing, with its high-pitched gable and strong-looking chimney, backed up by the smaller gable jutting out from the main roof.

The gable ends of the cottages, without showing much variety, differ in most instances from those in stone and other brick districts, by leaving out the projecting member of the coping. These flush-coped gables, with the bricks tailing into the wall three, four and even five times in its length, are peculiar to Norfolk and Suffolk. The general rule is to tail in the bricks at the springing, in the middle, and just below the apex, the portions between these triangular shapes being brick on edge. In the cottages near Filby Broad, Norfolk (page 54), the sloping buttress in the foreground shows brick quoins stretching into the flint at right angles to the

WESTON, SUFFOLK

48

WESTON, SUFFOLK

49

slope, a similar method to that which has been described. An interesting finish to the apex of a gable was noticed at Filby Broad: the bricks were laid on edge, but instead of finishing as a point, a cut brick was inserted, point downwards, in the triangular space left where the bricks on edge meet at the junction of the slopes. A small pedestal in brick was then built on the top, and finished with another brick at right angles to the face of the gable. The gables at Southwold, in Suffolk, and at Yarmouth, in

WALBERSWICK, SUFFOLK

Norfolk, are Dutch in character, and much the same in outline and treatment. At Southwold (below), in following the line of curves, the bricks are laid longitudinally and on the flat, and one curve overlaps the other—a reminiscence probably of the fantastic curves of Dutch stonework. At the junction of the concave ramp with the pedimental treatment of the top, the brick coping runs across the face of the gable, the end of the upper curve jutting beyond. At Yarmouth (page 55), the bricks are laid on edge and overlapping, not unlike that already noted in the finish of the arches over the doors and windows at Weston.

SOUTHWOLD, SUFFOLK

LOWESTOFT, SUFFOLK

51

There are a number of beautiful curved gables at Norwich, but in the villages along the coast of Suffolk and across the middle of Norfolk there are practically none, and only one example of the crow-stepped variety—just beyond Filby Broad—came under the notice of the writer. At Pulborough, in West Sussex, there is a crude form of crow-stepped gable in stone, each step chamfered on the upper edge. This form of gable is of brick origin, and suggests at once the need of steps, a bit of design directly inspired by the material. The ornamental iron wall ties were seldom absent from both the simple and curved gables, either in the form of an S or a long thin piece hammered into a heart-shape at both ends. There were sometimes two and even three in a gable, two about halfway up, and when a third was used it was placed just under the apex.

Perhaps the most characteristic feature of the cottages in Norfolk and Suffolk is the flint and brick wall. The flints are white and black, rough and rounded, the latter still known as cobbles or " petrified kidneys." Both the smooth and rough were used in a variety of ways. They might be ranged upright in rows, as in one of the group of cottages at Lowestoft, with the lighthouse showing above the trees in the background (page 51), or inclined to the right in one course, and to the left in the next. An uncommon method, suggestive of the galleting in Kent, was to alternate a row of brick headers with a row of flints all sloping in one direction. Another was an imitation of Flemish bond, the stretcher of brick, the space usually occupied by the header being filled in with flint. In some cottages at Lowestoft, opposite those seen in the admirable drawing on page 51, a very effective diaper of brick headers and flint was used, the quoins of the windows and the external angles of the dwelling being of brick. The brick headers at

KESSINGLAND, SUFFOLK

WALBERSWICK, SUFFOLK

53

Filby Broad (below) were introduced into the walling in a haphazard fashion ; and this seems to have been the most general custom.   The illustration of the gatehouse at Sandwich, in Kent (page 26), is an instance of the overlapping of the characteristics of two districts, the ground storey walling being a series of diapers of flint and stone, while the upper portion is weather boarded, and the roof is of small tiles.   Another method of using flint stone and brick was noticed in some boundary walling.   The base of the wall and the coping were of stone, the rest of the wall (about 8 feet high) was divided horizontally by a brick band of headers, placed midway in the height, another course of brick came under the stone coping, while stretchers and headers built in alternate courses divided the wall vertically into squares, the filling-in being of flint.   The tower on the ramparts at Yarmouth, in Norfolk, is a remarkable example of the use of flint and stone, the upper portion being divided horizontally and vertically by projecting bands of stone, and the square faces between are of black flints. These black flints were used a great deal in this form of inlaid work, but more often in the churches than in the cottage dwellings.

About all this walling there is a playful and almost casual handling of materials that yields the same happy results as those obtained in the use of other methods and other materials by the builders in Kent and Surrey ; and in both cases the tendency is to reach effects by the use of a variety of

FILBY BROAD, NORFOLK

YARMOUTH, NORFOLK

55

material and colour—quite the reverse of the means adopted by the stone-masons in the Cotswold Hills, where the results are attained by practically one material.

Norfolk, Suffolk and Essex also are rich in good ornamental plaster-work, more especially in the Suffolk villages. At Stanstead and Clare, for instance, there are some fine examples of this external decoration. Mr. Reginald Blomfield, in his history of the Renaissance in England, finds an English and foreign tendency in the plaster-work of the sixteenth century, the first being attributed to the English workmen, and the other the result of employing Dutch and German workmen. The principal motive in this design consists in variations of strapwork, and to this influence may be attributed the work at Stanstead and other villages in the same district. An interesting example is the front of the houses at Clare, in Suffolk. The elevation of the ground-floor storey is covered with scroll-work on a geometrical basis, and the upper storeys and gables with a running pattern ; and a similar pattern forms the frieze between the two storeys. A cottage at Wyvenhoe, near Colchester, in Suffolk, has a playful interpretation of the same work.

It is divided into panels and filled with a scroll-like pattern and interlacing foliage, suggesting the ingenious work of a German smith. Mr. G. T. Robinson, in his preface to Mr. William Millar's work on plastering, quotes an interesting reference to this almost extinct plaster-work or stucco : "Some men will have their walls plastered, some pargetted and white-limed, some rough-cast, some pricked, some wrought with plaster-of-Paris." The pricked work is probably the method still used sometimes in the county of Essex. A great amount of plaster-work was done in these districts at the beginning of the sixteenth century and onward, the surfaces diapered and stamped with all kinds of patterns, produced probably by pressing wooden or metal tools into the plaster when moist. "About this time," says Mr. Robinson, "the plasterer's and pargettor's art and craft had now become of such importance that it was formed into a separate guild and company in London, in 1501, by

YARMOUTH, NORFOLK

YARMOUTH, NORFOLK

57

Henry VII., who granted them 'the right to search, and try and make and exercise due search as well, in, upon, and of all manner of stuff touching and concerning the art and mystery of pargettors, commonly called plaisterers, and upon all work and workmen in the said art and mystery, so that the said work might be just, true and lawful, without any deceit or fraud whatsoever.'" The steep pantile roofs of the cottages in Norfolk and Suffolk were probably in the first place copied by the same workmen who thatched the stately and dignified barns in these counties. Unlike the majority of modern workmen, the villagers and the craftsmen of the small towns did not always follow the same occupation all the year round. At one season a man was building, at another probably engaged in bringing in the harvest and thatching the hayricks, and shaping them on the lines 'of the cottage buildings. It has been noticed by some authorities that the measurements of the ricks and the cottages

occasionally tally almost exactly. At first sight this seems preposterous, but nothing could have been more natural to the craftsman than to follow the shapes and measurements with which he was familiar. And it may well be that the barn builders were the cottage builders also. It was of common occurrence that a man followed many trades in the country districts. In the records of Barnstaple Church there is mention of one, David Bedman by name, who worked at tiling, rung the bells, cleaned the pillars and walls of the church, made Communion bread, and cleaned the churchyard. In our grandfathers' time, and even now in some country districts, it is possible to find men who are able to turn from one occupation to another. A remarkable instance of this versatility came under the notice of the present writer in a Devonshire village. A man was skilled in the making of both furniture and violins ; and not only could he make these things, but he could make them well. In another case, in Staffordshire, one of the workmen could lay a floor, repair walling and brickwork, make farm gates, thatch a roof, and thresh. It is significant, that in districts where thatch is the prevailing covering for the roof, that the same method of keeping the thatch in place on the hayricks is still adopted. An interesting detail in

58

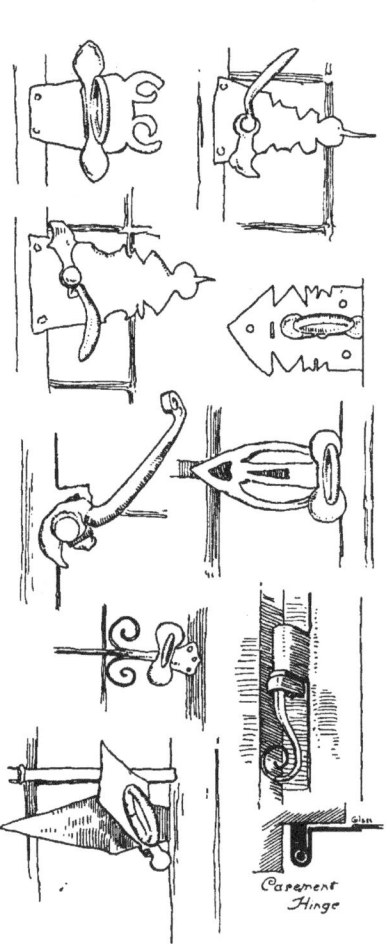

CASEMENT FITTINGS

connection with the ricks of East Suffolk and West Norfolk are the finials at either end, made out of the thatching material; they resemble an opening flower on the end of a long stem.

The barns, to which we have referred, are covered with the most decorative thatching of any district in England. The shaping of the edges, of the double cresting over the ridge, and of the edges down the roof when carried out in a series of slopes, extend the whole length of a big barn, and form certainly one of the most beautiful objects in the landscape. Imagine for a moment the yellow-green undulating plains stretching away as far as the eye can reach, brilliant red patches of poppies here and there, the large church towers, the upstanding sails of the ships that float on the unseen rivers, and then these occasional black weather-boarded buildings covered with thatch running from end to end, with the edges cut and shaped in all manner of scolloping and other patterns.

Although it is extremely difficult to determine to what extent the Flemings influenced the architecture of the villages and the cottages, it was probably less in Norfolk and Suffolk than is usually assumed. For instance, chimneys, a feature where one would naturally expect some details of definite Flemish character, there are none to prove their skill in brick building. There are one or two crude examples of circular plan at Blythburgh, and another variety at Walberswick (page 50), but for the most part the chimneys are disappointing, and generally finish with a double course of projecting bricks. Another detail, the dormer, with roof of flatter pitch than the main roof, may be foreign, but seems more likely to have arisen from the difficulty of covering a small gabled or hipped roof with pantiles. The most remarkable point illustrated by these dwellings is the wonderful conservatism with which the builders clung to their methods of using materials; as, for example, in the high-pitched gable, with its iron ties and monograms, and the simplicity characteristic of English work which persisted from generation to generation. The Englishman is generally provincial and hates new ways, like Coggan, Thomas Hardy's rustic. Says he: "I won't say much for myself, but I've never changed a single doctrine. I've stuck like a plaster to the old faith I was born in. I hate a fellow who'll change his old ancient doctrines for the sake of getting to heaven. I'd as soon turn King's evidence for the few pounds you get." Of a piece with this religious constancy are the remarks of Mr. Poyser in "Adam Bede." He says: "I'm none for worretting," rising from his chair and walking slowly towards the door, "but I should be loath to leave the old place and the parish where I was bred and born and father before me."

WHITBOURNE, HEREFORDSHIRE. FROM A WATER-COLOUR DRAWING BY E. A. CHADWICK.

DIVISION III.

CHESHIRE, SHROPSHIRE HEREFORDSHIRE

WHITBOURNE, HEREFORDSHIRE. FROM A WATER-COLOUR DRAWING BY E. A. CHADWICK.

DIVISION III.

CHESHIRE, SHROPSHIRE
HEREFORDSHIRE

III.—CHESHIRE, SHROPSHIRE AND HEREFORDSHIRE

N O two districts could illustrate with more point the variety of types in the English cottage than the counties on the east coast north of the Thames, and those of Cheshire, Shropshire and Herefordshire. The remarkable contrast between them is more than one of detail, for neither the materials nor the construction are the same, and in the general effect there can be no comparison whatsoever. The one is simple both in form and construction, the other rich in effect and more complicated in structure. The one is chiefly red on the landscape, the other chiefly black-and-white. The one has steep roofs, the other steep and flat. Those to the east are little known, those towards the north-west are well known. To the great majority of the public, the study of architecture is generally of little interest, but these cottages of black-and-white, more especially those of Cheshire, have always found a place in the heart of the incorrigibly sentimental Englishman.

More generally known than those of any other counties, they have been freely imitated with a wanton disregard for the real origin of their charm. The picture painter, the scene painter, the man in the street, the man who lives in the suburbs, and last but not least the speculative builder with romantic tendencies, are all united in their admiration; and truth to say, this lively preference for the obvious in cottage architecture

NETHER ALDERLEY, CHESHIRE

63

is easier to understand than the attitude of the architect who rhapsodises over them, and yet on the first opportunity feebly plants on the plaster-work of his client's house a few thin upright and cross pieces and dignifies it by the name of half-timbering. Architects and their clients started with the placid assumption that these half-timbered cottages could be built without the necessity of using the original methods of construction. In no buildings has the construction been so deliberately made the foundation of all that was interesting and beautiful in their design as in these old cottages, for with the exception of the small pieces of wood that helped to form the geometrical patterns and diapers of black-and-white, no timbers were introduced except for some definite work in holding the building together. Whether the result was to be simple or elaborate, it was always based on the main lines of the construction ; nothing, therefore, could be more ludicrous than to imagine that this system of building might be copied by planting on the plaster these boards, or by whitewashing brickwork, and mimicking the timber by painting. The beauty of the old cottages was more than skin deep, or rather more than the depth of paint and one-inch boards.

In the south of Cheshire, the painting of the white-washed brickwork with vertical and horizontal black stripes is the favourite method of restoring, and very often the timbers are not even correctly copied. If such things are done in the name of restoration, it is almost impossible to ex-pect that new buildings will fare any better. The fact is, no cottages are so difficult to build as those in the spirit of the old timber-and-plaster dwell-ings, and yet no style has been cribbed more often, and with such disastrous results. In view of this popular if questionable ap-preciation, it is strange how little the originals have been looked after. Timbers have been covered with plaster-work, or superseded by neat brickwork, carving has been damaged or re-moved altogether, and stone roofs have been taken

CHESTER, CHESHIRE

64

ALDERLEY EDGE, CHESHIRE

65

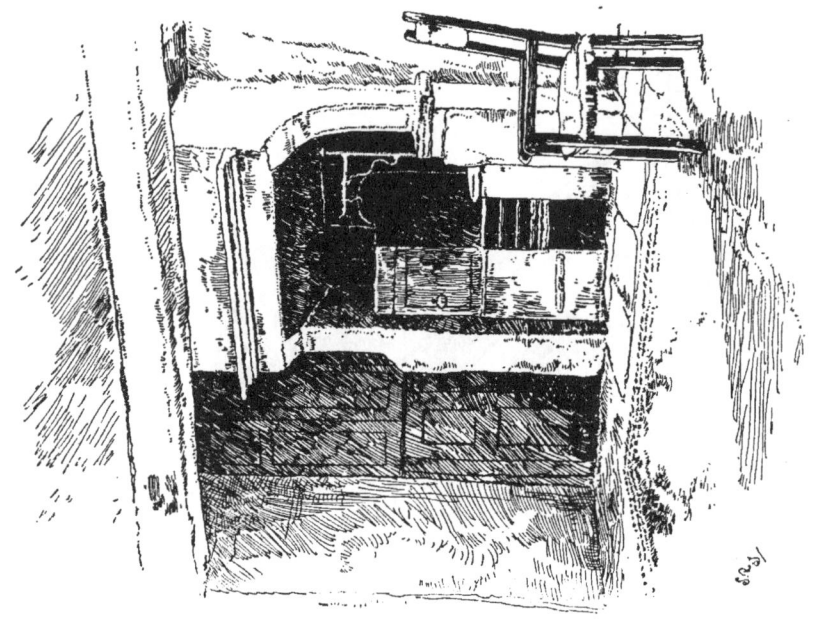

ALDERLEY EDGE, CHESHIRE

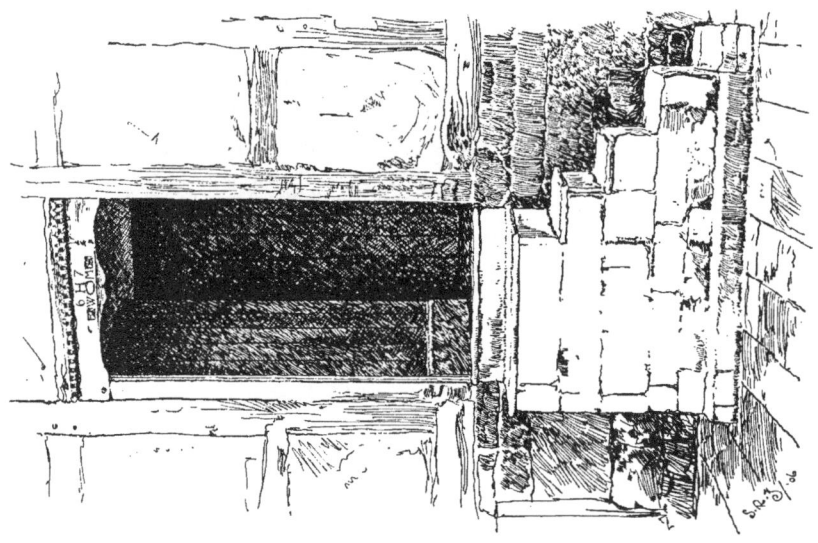

CONGLETON, CHESHIRE

SANDBACH, CHESHIRE

off and covered with the common thin slates of ordinary manufacture.

The same method of construction used in the large halls is followed in the cottages. There is the same low wall, often of tool-marked masonry, the stones as much as three feet long, one foot deep and ten inches wide; and the tool marks always from the middle towards the outer edges, sometimes in two directions, at others in four; if in two, from the middle to the top and bottom edges; if in four, towards the four outer corners of the stone. This only occurs when the masonry is built of large stones worked fairly smooth, as in the cottage near Prestbury (opposite), but in other instances the wall is of rough and irregularly coursed stones, comparatively small, with the large bonding stones at the angles and in the walls of the chimneys. The height of the wall varies. At Much Wenlock many of the buildings are stone up to the first-floor level, but the general rule is two to three feet, the wood

PRESTBURY, CHESHIRE

67

framing being set back about an inch to two inches. The stone base of the corner house at Much Wenlock (below) is only about eighteen inches from the level of the ground to the framing, and even lower where the ground rises. A part of the house to the left is built entirely of stone, and probably is of later date. These additions, wholly of stone or of brickwork, and often white-washed, occur frequently and with the most happy results. At Prestbury village, in Cheshire, for example, some of the half-timbered dwellings are side-by-side with others of this white-washed character, the wood frames of the windows set in a little way, with the wide leads of the transomed windows painted white. The contrast is a pleasant one, and a happy relief from the black timbers of the other cottages. The windows of many of them are opened and shut with window-fasteners of fascinating design.

It has been said that the chief characteristics of these cottages and large timber buildings are their geometrical patterning within the main timbers, the heavy scantlings of the woodwork and the flat pitch of the roofs. These details are a more incidental than essential feature of the style. Much of the patterning of the more elaborate examples in Cheshire could be omitted, as it has been to a large extent in Shropshire and Oxfordshire. The scantlings of the half-timber work are not always heavy, and the roofs were probably, many of them, originally thatched. It is true that a number of the gables have the flat pitch necessary for heavy stone slates, but the majority are at an angle suitable for thatching. Moreover, those

MUCH WENLOCK, SHROPSHIRE

MUCH WENLOCK, SHROPSHIRE

69

which are thatched suggest that it is the material for timber cottages, like those at Bromfield, in Shropshire (below), the cottage at Alderley Edge, in Cheshire (page 65), and the Boar Inn at Sandbach, in Cheshire. The chief characteristics are the methods of construction, which have already been detailed in Mr. E. A. Ould's interesting notes on timber buildings. He says: "Stout oak sills are laid horizontally upon a low wall of stone or brick, and into these are tenoned upright posts, the larger ones being placed at the external angles. Upon these upright posts, horizontal heads are placed just below the level of the chamber floor, and the intervening spaces formed into panels with thinner pieces, the whole being framed and tenoned together and pinned with oak pins. The joists of the floor are then laid, resting upon the horizontal heads, and frequently being partly supported by internal beams, which appear in the ceilings of the house. Upon the ends of the joists the sill of the upper storey is laid, and the framing is, more or less, a repetition of that below, the head forming a support for the spars of the roof, and being frequently carried over at the ends as a wall plate to carry the overhanging gables." Where timber ridges occur they are generally directly beneath the rafters and placed anglewise. The sizes of the timbers vary considerably. At Alderley Edge some of the angle posts measure 8 ins. and 9 ins. square, and the other timbers 7 ins. and 8 ins. on the face, the wooden pegs pinning them together project $\frac{3}{4}$ in. and of the same diameter. They appear to be slightly wedge-shaped, probably to allow for the tightening up of the framing when the usual and inevitable shrinkage had taken place after exposure to wind and weather. The panels between the framing are of brickwork, which here, as in many other cases, project. This may be due to the shrinkage of the timber, for it is sometimes flush in the same building. When the panels

BROMFIELD, SHROPSHIRE

70

CULMINGTON, SHROPSHIRE

71

are of plaster, they "are filled in with a basket-work osier foundation, daubed over with clay strengthened with straw or stringy weeds. The finishing coat is of plaster on both sides, richly matted with hair, and frequently set back half an inch or more."[1] In the panels of a cottage at Alderley Edge, the woodwork is arranged in the form of diapers—the plaster squares alternating with the wood—and pinned into the cross-pieces and uprights. In the same cottage the pattern occurs in diamond-shaped panels in the gable. The general effect is rich and barbaric, a characteristic noticeable in the carving and the gouge cuts on the barge boards and brackets. Many of the details recall the work of savage races, such, for instance, as the zig-zag cuttings on the windows in Church Street, Ledbury, the brackets and barge boards at Middlebrook, the scolloping of the edges of the beam on the gables at Alderley Edge. Another characteristic bit of detail is the doorway at Congleton in Cheshire (page 66), with its shaped lintel, the initials and date in the middle, the enriching of the beam over the lintel with scolloping in the middle member, and dentils beneath. The timbers as they get nearer the top of the buildings are filled in with the geometrical patterns, like those in the gable at Prestbury (page 67). The large spaces between some of the timbers is generally an alteration or restoration filled in with brick. The illustrations of the cottages at Alderley Edge, Prestbury, and Sandbach (pages 65 and 67) are all typical of the elaborate patterning. Directly Shropshire is approached, the timbering becomes less playful and more in vertical and horizontal lines—as, for instance, at Craven Arms (page 73). The corner posts are generally thicker than the rest, and strutted. Among some of the geometrical patterns are the diamond and the quatrefoil, while at Alderley Edge the curved pieces of wood in the cove are pierced in the form of a cross. Another fine example is

BROMFIELD, SHROPSHIRE

[1] "Old Halls in Lancashire and Cheshire," by Henry Tayler.

...th a basket-work osier foundation,
...with straw or stringy weeds. The
...sides, richly matted with hair, and
...." In the panels of a cottage at
...ged in the form of diapers—the
...wood—and pinned into the cross-pieces
...the pattern occurs in diamond-shaped
...is rich and barbaric, a characteristic
...cuts on the barge boards and brackets.
...of savage races, such, for instance, as
in Church Street, Ledbury, the brackets
...be scolloping of the edges of the beam
...Another characteristic bit of detail is
...ire (page 66), with its shaped lintel, the
...enriching of the beam over the lintel
..., and dentils beneath. The timbers
...kings are filled in with the geometrical

BROMFIELD, SHROPSHIRE

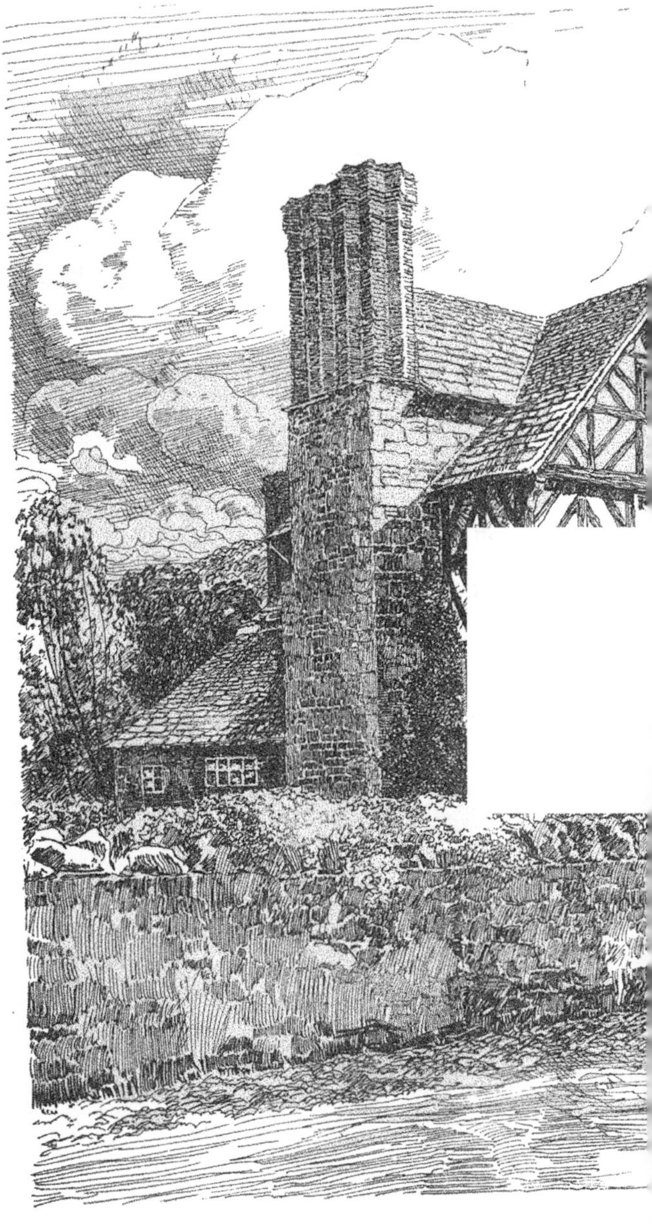

CRAV

HARTON, SHROPSHIRE

74

that at Prestbury, in Cheshire (page 67). An interesting detail noticeable in the chimney of this cottage is the drip in stepped brick, a common enough detail in Worcestershire and Warwickshire. In Herefordshire and Shropshire the timbers are not so close together, nor is there the same tendency to run to pattern as in Cheshire. Many of the cottages, in fact, have a near relationship to those in the South-Eastern counties, although generally the construction is much in advance of the majority in Kent or Surrey. This superiority was due to two reasons, first, to the fact that, unlike Kent and Surrey, where bricks and tiles were used as much as wood, in Cheshire, Shropshire and Herefordshire wood was the chief material ; and, secondly, to the influence of that remarkable man John Abel, the carpenter-architect of Hereford. With him, as with the other little known cottage builders of these counties, the terms " to build " and " to timber " were synonymous.

This carpenter exercised considerable influence in his own county and in Shropshire. His work is restrained, and shows a careful consideration for the right spacing of the timbers, which places it much above the over - elaborated Cheshire fronts. Nothing could be more effective than the zigzag disposition of timbers on the Market House at Ledbury, being both decorative and constructive. The examples at Pembridge (pages 77 and 78), and Orleton (page 79), in Herefordshire, and the Reader's House at Ludlow, in Shropshire, are either his work or influenced by him. He lived to the age of ninety-seven, and a few years before his death made his own monument, engraved his own effigy and those of his two wives, and the

LEY, HEREFORDSHIRE

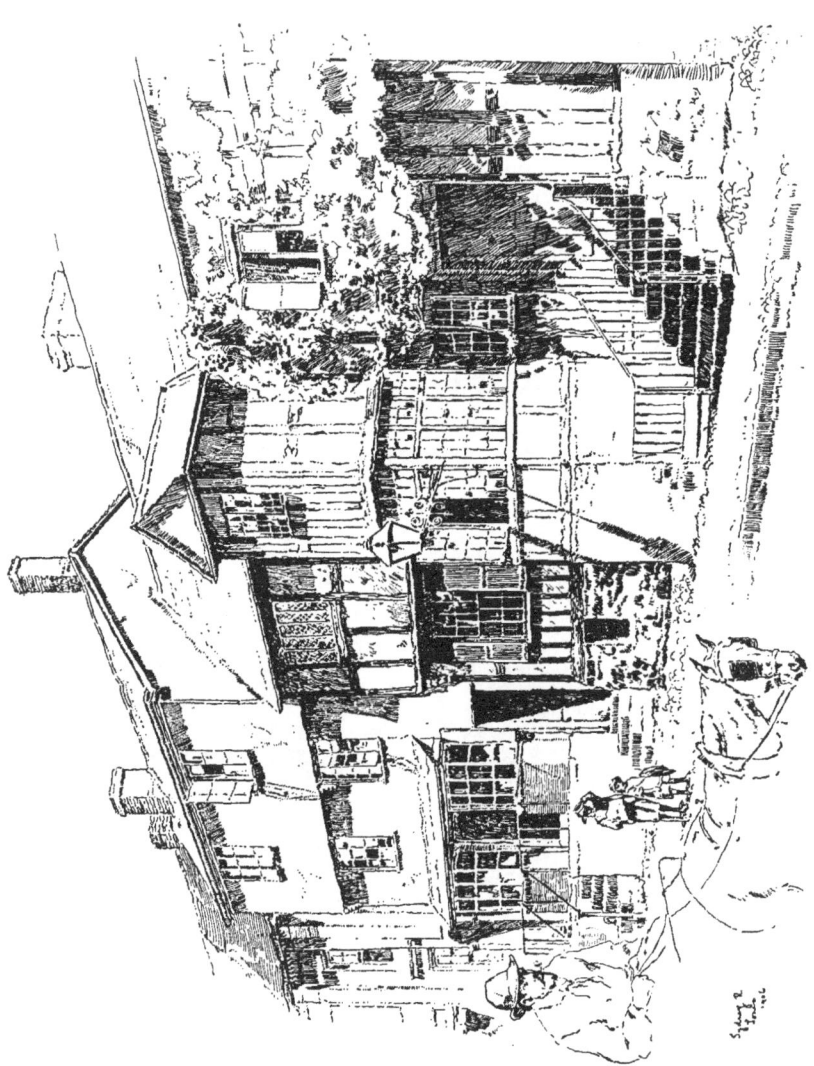

LEDBURY, HEREFORDSHIRE

76

PEMBRIDGE, HEREFORDSHIRE

77

symbols of his occupation, the rule, the compass, and the square, and, alas! wrote his own epitaph, as follows:—

> " This craggy stone a covering is for an architect's bed,
> That lofty buildings raised high, yet now lies down his head,
> This line and rule, so Death concludes, are locked up in store,
> Build they who list or they who wist, for he can build no more.
> His house of clay could hold no longer,
> May Heaven's—frame him a stronger.   JOHN ABEL.
> Vive ut vivas in vitam æternam." [1]

The esteem in which the known man, John Abel the carpenter, was held in Hereford and the immediate district is only one instance of the important position generally occupied by the unknown village carpenter or smith. It is certain that the local craftsman was by no means the negligible factor in the village life that he is to-day. His position was often an official one, his pay coming to him through grants of land, and while many of the trades or crafts were hereditary, the trades connected with commerce and the supplying of goods from distant markets were not so. Those who produced, those who built the walls, hammered the gates, and chiselled the wood were the privileged folk of the village community, and not those who were merely a superior kind of pedlar like the modern manufacturer. Amongst savages the smith was one of the most important members of the tribe, and the number of village inns called after the principal trades or crafts is another instance of the important position the mason, smith and carpenter held in the village. It is probable that in addition to gathering at the inn for convivial meetings, they settled points of detail and construction over their tankards of beer. The chimneys of the cottages in Cheshire have not much character, but in Shropshire

PEMBRIDGE, HEREFORDSHIRE

[1] "Ancient Timber Edifices of England," by John Clayton, A.R.I.B.A.

78

ORLETON, HEREFORDSHIRE

79

there are examples almost equal to those in Kent. At Craven Arms (page 73) there is a remarkably fine one with well-proportioned rick shafts springing from the large projection carried up in stone. b At Whitbourne, in Herefordshire (opposite page 61), there is an interesting chimney in brick, with an unusual cap connecting two shafts of different design. A peculiar feature was noticed at Wellington. The projecting V-shapes on the shaft were abruptly finished square a few courses below the capping, and suggested that the bricklayer felt he was unable to mitre his capping round the projection. In another unusual group of shafts in this village there are five flues, the middle one placed anglewise and the others attached to each of its sides, thus forming a star-shaped plan of plain, square shafts, which rise off a square stone base. The same plan occurs at Cressage. Besides the timber cottages in these counties there are some rough-cast examples with beautiful thatched roofs; and on the moors between Buxton and Macclesfield, on the borders of Derbyshire and Cheshire, are a number of whitewashed dwellings. These are simple, crude rough-stone structures, with plain square chimneys of the same material, and the roofs covered with stone slates; the mouldings, if any, are of the most primitive character, and the walls either lime-whited or left untouched. The moorlands on each side of the steep road that leads out of Buxton (also in the direction of the inn called "The Cat and Fiddle," and from there down into Macclesfield) are dotted here and there with these single cottages and farm buildings.

To follow this building tradition in preference to that of the more usual wood and timber dwellings in the same county, would seem to be most in harmony with the geological formations of the north. In Derbyshire to the east, and Lancashire to the north of Cheshire, stone is the prevailing material and is used in a somewhat similar, though at the same time more elaborate, manner than is usual on the moors.

EARDISLAND, HEREFORDSHIRE

EARDISLAND, HEREFORDSHIRE

81

LONG WITTENHAM, OXFORDSHIRE. FROM A WATER-COLOUR DRAWING BY WILFRID BALL, R.E.

GLOUCESTERSHIRE, ON
DERBYSHIRE, NORTHA\

DIVISION IV.

GLOUCESTERSHIRE, OXFORDSHIRE, DERBYSHIRE, NORTHAMPTONSHIRE

IV.—GLOUCESTERSHIRE, OXFORD-SHIRE, DERBYSHIRE AND NORTH-AMPTONSHIRE.

THE charm of the Cotswold cottage and village is unique. The wonderfully quiet and mellow beauty is best appreciated, perhaps, on first entering a village or hamlet towards the evening. Often at the foot of the hills the approach is made under ideal conditions. Half-way down the incline glimpses are caught between the trees of grey and yellow stone walls, and to the right and left the ground rises and curves gently upward in long stretches of rolling upland, covered with waving corn ripe for the harvest, alternating with green fields and patches of newly-turned-up soil. Behind the village there is a red wafer sun in a sky the colour of lead, and as the visitor draws near, the many gables and chimneys stand out in sharp silhouette. The hills round about are touched with the sombre glow of

WELFORD-ON-AVON, GLOUCESTERSHIRE

85

the vanishing sun, while here and there the chimney of a cottage and the tower of the church are splashed with ruddy light. The hollows in the hills are in shadow, birds are asleep, the villagers at rest, and everywhere there broods that intense stillness of departing day, broken by the faint and melancholy sound of the breeze blowing across the fields of corn. In the glare of the morning sunlight the village is different, but its fascination remains the same, for, like all great work, it has the power to stamp upon the mind and heart that distinct and lasting impression which only strong and simple nature can give.

With the exception perhaps of Yorkshire, and parts of Lancashire, there are no counties in which the cottages are so characteristically English as those up and down the Cotswold Hills. They are all offsprings of the spirit which hovers about the moors of Yorkshire and Lancashire, of Wuthering Heights and of lonely Egdon Heath. Stone is used throughout—stone for the walls, stone for the windows, and stone for the roofs. They can generally be dated between the latter part of the sixteenth and the end of the following century. In the earlier buildings there is a distinct Gothic feeling akin to the Perpendicular work of the previous century, particularly noticeable in buildings like the almshouses at Campden, in Gloucestershire (page 93), the house and shop at Burford, in Oxfordshire (page 104), and the entrance at Rothwell, in Northamptonshire (page 106). This mediæval character never disappeared entirely, although there crept into the details and mouldings some of the classic forms

WELFORD-ON-AVON, GLOUCESTERSHIRE

WELFORD-ON-AVON, GLOUCESTERSHIRE

87

which had already become the current design of the larger towns. The parapet of the cottage at Weston-sub-Edge (page 90) is probably a Renaissance innovation, and is found again at Burford, in Oxfordshire, in the dwellings of a more classic character. But fashions in details might come and might go, the heart of the Cotswolds was mediæval and always retained in its essentials the villagers' expression of the middle ages. And just as long as the builders of these cottages remained in close touch with their materials and the villages in which they first saw the light, this spirit dwelt in their work. The late examples in Campden and Mickleton are clothed with new mouldings and newer forms, but the spirit and the methods are the same. There is no other district in England that has expressed so simply and so beautifully in terms of building the unity between the soil, the dwelling, and its inhabitants. The spell of the severe outlines, the fascination and charm of the simple details, the quaint fancy and the appearance of strength suggested by the stone walls and slate roofs, are full of a magic that no number of visits can dispel. These men from the Cotswold District knew instinctively the value of

the rightly-placed ornament and the accumulation of well-proportioned parts to form a unity of expression, and the place for simplicity and the position for playfulness. Their strong individuality is shown in the design of the kneelers at the foot of the gables, in the finials, and the tablets (page 165), containing the names or initials and date of those who occupied and possibly built the cottages; they even show the changes of occupants. Many of them are admirable and complete little masterpieces of well-cut lettering. Names in full occur on some, and others in addition bear a quaint legend or device. The arrangement of the

WELFORD-ON-AVON, GLOUCESTERSHIRE

88

█t design of the larger towns.
█b-Edge (page 90) is probably
█ again at Burford, in Oxford-
classic character. But fashions in
the heart of the Cotswolds was
█tials the villagers' expression of
█ as the builders of these cottages
█terials and the villages in which
It in their work. The late examples
e█ with new mouldings and newer
█ are the same. There is no other
█ simply and so beautifully in terms
il, the dwelling, and its inhabitants.
fascination and charm of the simple
█ce of strength suggested by the stone
c that no number of visits can dispel.
ict : new instinctively the value of

IVOS, GLOUCESTERSHIRE

the in late ages. And those who
remained in close touch with their materials and the village
they first saw the light, this spirit runs in their work. The late examples
in Campden and Mickleton are a series with new mouldings and newer
forms, but the spirit and the outlines are the same. There is no other
district in England that ... simply and so beautifully in terms
of building the unity between ... dwelling, and its inhabitants.
The spell of the severe outlines, the ... and charm of the simple
details, the quaint fancy and the appearance of strength suggested by the stone
walls and slate roofs, are full of a magic that no number of visits can dispel.
These men from the Cotswold District ... instinctively the value of

the rightly-placed
ornament and the
accumulation of well
proportioned parts
form a unity of ex-
pression, and the place
for simplicity and the
position for playful-
ness. Their strong in-
dividuality is shown
in the design of the
kneelers at the foot
of the gable, the old
finials, and the gable
(page 165), contain-
ing the names or
initials and date of
those who occupied
and probably built the
cottages; they even
show the ... of

them are admirable

masterpieces of well-
cut lettering.
in full occur on some,
and others in addition
bear a quaint legend

TEWKESBURY, GLOUCESTERSHIRE.   FROM A WATER-COLOUR DRAWING BY WILMOT PILSBURY, R.W.S.

WELFORD-ON-AVON, GLOUCESTERSHIRE

89

WESTON-SUB-EDGE, GLOUCESTERSHIRE

WELFORD-ON-AVON, GLOUCESTERSHIRE

90

WESTON-SUB-EDGE, GLOUCESTERSHIRE

lettering alters considerably, the later ones being freer in treatment; their spacing is charming, and no two are alike. The tablet at Stanton (page 165), dated 1604, with the names "John, James," nicely arranged below the date, is a good type of one of these well-proportioned panels; less careful and more fanciful is the one at Minster Lovel (page 165), with the initials "H.H.," and dated 1694. There is one at Matlock on the Wheatsheaf Inn that suggests the wheat.

The walling is full of variety in Derbyshire; the large size of the stone-dressed quoins is characteristic, and measures as much as 2 ft. long, 12 ins. deep, and 5 ins. on the bed. The doorway at Youlgreave (page 110) is a typical specimen, with roughly chamfered edge on the jambs, the head being left square. In some the faced edges are carefully dressed for an inch and the rest slightly boasted and often crudely honeycombed. Others are chiselled in definite lines along the length of the stone. Another method was roughly to smooth the stone, dress the edges for an inch, and work the rest of the stone as if a comb had been drawn across it. This applies only to the dressings, the rest of the walling was more or less rough, and in some of the cottages stones here and there projected as much as 6 ins. without being squared off. All the work in Youlgreave is coarse, the panels of doors and windows often set forward an inch beyond the wall face, and in some instances considerably more. The entrance to a cottage at Bakewell (page 108) shows this characteristic. In the example at Taddington (page 113)

CAMPDEN, GLOUCESTERSHIRE

92

CAMPDEN, GLOUCESTERSHIRE

93

the stone head and sill of the windows are continued as much as 9 ins. beyond the outer line of the jambs, a method of construction made necessary by the small width of the stone that was carried up without any bonding into the walling, except at the top and the bottom. This primitive arrangement is common in both Derbyshire and Lancashire, where the ordinary walling was also built round the windows without any dressing whatsoever, in the same way as at Ebrington, in Gloucestershire (page 101); the lintels and sills (if any) were of wood. The same feature occurs in Oxfordshire. At Chipping Campden the stones of the masonry are dressed with a good deal of care and laid evenly in courses of varying depth, or in deep bands alternating with narrow ones. The walling at Rothwell, in Northamptonshire (page 106), is built in this way. It is noticeable that in many cottages the stones of the masonry are of larger dimensions in the lower part of the building, and then, as if to guard against a too sudden transition to smaller work an occasional deep band is introduced into the thinner courses. At Bibury, one of the most beautiful villages in Gloucestershire (pages 96 and 97), where the ordinary roughly coursed masonry is almost universal, one of the chimney gables is banded with smooth-dressed masonry, and pigeon-holes are introduced in others with a thin projecting course of stone beneath. These stone bands occur again at Little Rissington and in some farm buildings outside Burford. A variation of the dry walling used so much for the gardens, fences, and the divisions between the fields, occurs both here and at Burford. Instead of being constructed in the usual way, entirely without mortar, three and four jointed courses are alternated with six or seven dry.

UPPER GUITING, GLOUCESTERSHIRE

94

In all the varieties of walling there are none that show mere cleverness. When a change occurs, it is for some obvious reason. It might be quarried in block, or it might be in thin layers, or courses of red iron stone might alternate with those of limestone ; but whatever method was followed, it was determined very largely by the local quarry. It was not invariably so, for the carefully dressed stone in the majority of chimney shafts and in the bay windows occur side by side with ordinary walling in the rest of the cottage. Large stones were generally used, too, for the jambs of the stone dormers. Before a satisfactory treatment of this feature was accomplished it went through three developments, not necessarily arising out of each other, but gradual improvements that might occur in one village and not in another, even where the rest of the work was of a superior character. At Chipping Campden, for instance, where perhaps there is the best masonry, the early dormer is general, while at Bibury, where the masonry is not so carefully finished, the dormer has blossomed into one of a thoroughly stone character. The original dormer was a copy of the wood and plaster type common in the adjoining counties, such as those at Broadway, in Worcester-

shire (page 119), and at Ducklington, in Oxfordshire (page 103). It was not an exact reproduction, the tile roof of Warwickshire and Wor-cestershire changing into one of slate as in the Cotswold counties. This survival of form, change of material, and general overlapping of types is particularly characteristic of the cottage at Broadway (page 119). Another interest-ing detail is the coping at Weston-sub-Edge (page 90); a rather unusual arrangement was adopted, the walls were coped, the gables running out without any coping. The absence of this detail in so many of the small gables probably grew out of these modifications of the original dormers. Instead of wood frames, stone mullions were adopted, and the plaster cheeks and filling-in over the windows were avoided by run-ning the roof down to the eaves level, as at Upper Swell (page 102), Upper Guiting

BIBURY, GLOUCESTERSHIRE

96

BIBURY, GLOUCESTERSHIRE

97

STANTON, GLOUCESTERSHIRE

STANTON, GLOUCESTERSHIRE

WELFORD-ON-AVON, GLOUCESTERSHIRE. FROM A WATER-COLOUR DRAWING BY WILFRID BALL, R.E.

NORTHLEACH, GLOUCESTERSHIRE

99

ARLINGTON, GLOUCESTERSHIRE
100

EBRINGTON, GLOUCESTERSHIRE

(page 94), and Arlington (page 100), forming a gable rising from the face of the cottage. This is peculiar to Bibury and the surrounding neighbourhood, and is only occasionally seen in the north of Gloucestershire. The village of Willersey (page 95) shows dormers with and without coping, and raised very little above the stone slates, there being no bye-laws requiring that they should be 15 ins. above the roof. The group of cottages at Bibury are remarkably fine examples of the simpler work in Gloucestershire. A characteristic detail is the weathering at the base of the chimney in the gable end (page 97), which follows the same pitch as the gable, like the examples at Stanton (page 98); but in some cottages, like those at Chedworth, Arlington and Gretton, it is taken straight across. At the Post Office, Weston-sub-Edge (page 91), the gable coping is continued up the face of the chimney the width of its projection from the wall. The arrangement of the flues is generally in the form of a square or oblong stack, but there are instances in which the plan is that of a cross, and in others placed anglewise, as in the almshouses at Campden (page 93). A small space is left between them and the two shafts, connected at the top by the necking and capping, and at the bottom by the base.

The doorways and door heads are very varied; on many of them the builders lavished all their knowledge of detail, as at Willersey, Broadway, Aldsworth, Stow-on-the-Wold (page 162). The first one has come under the influence of classic forms, and the example at Aldsworth (page 162) shows a stone head supported on wood corbels; this may be a restoration, but certainly appears to be original. The finial on the gable is another detail to which a great amount of attention was given. That at Stanton (page 165) is a usual type of quite Gothic character, while the one at Arlington (page 165) is classic in feeling. Some of the doorways show the influence of the Perpendicular style, with double

UPPER SWELL, GLOUCESTERSHIRE

█ g a gable rising from the face of
█ and the surrounding neighbourhood,
north of Gloucestershire. The village
█ with and without coping, and raised
█ being no bye-laws requiring that
█. The group of cottages at Bibury are
█er work in Gloucestershire. A charac-
█e base of the chimney in the gable
█e pitch as the gable, like the examples
█e cottages, like those at Chedworth,
straight across. At the Post Office,
█e coping is continued up the face of the
█ from the wall. The arrangement of
█ square or oblong stack, but there are
of a cross, and in others placed angle-
█den (page 93). A small space is left
connected at the top by the necking

█WELL, GLOUCESTERSHIRE

...way little above the stone slates, there being no bye-laws re... they should be 13 ft. above the roof. The group of cottages a... remarkably fine examples of the simpler work in Gloucestershire... teristic detail is the weathering at the base of the chimney i... end (page 93), which follows the same pitch as the gable, like t... in some cottages, like those at... taken straight across. At the... he gable coping is continued up th... projection from the wall. The ar... the flues is generally in the form of a square or oblong stack, b... instances in which the plan is that of a cross, and in others p... wise as in the almshouses at Campden (page 93). A small... between them and the two shafts, connected at the top by... and capping, and at the... bottom by the base

The doorways and door heads are very varied, on many of them the builder lavished all that an outlet of detail, as in fine years, Broadway, ... Stow-on-the-World (page 162). The last one has come under the influence of classic forms, and the example at Aldsworth (page 162) shows a stone head supported on wood corbels: this may be a restoration, but certainly appears to be original. The finial on the gable is another detail to which a great amount of attention was given. That at Stanton (page 165) is a usual type of quite Gothic character, while the one at Ashing-ton (page 149) is ...

LONG WITTENHAM, OXFORDSHIRE.   FROM A WATER-COLOUR DRAWING BY WILFRID BALL, R.E.

DUCKLINGTON, OXFORDSHIRE

103

mouldings and a fillet between the inner moulding following the line of the four-centre arch, and the other taken up and carried across square. Notwithstanding the variety of simple detail, the flights of fancy are practically confined to these doors, the finials, the tablets, and the metal-work. Chimneys, windows, and mouldings are repeated time after time with little variation, and the fenestration of windows and disposition of the masses of masonry seldom indicate any new and startling departure. The builders kept to the well-beaten track of tradition; what was good enough for the father was good enough for the son. Everything tended to unity of effect; and this, perhaps more than their picturesqueness, is the distinctive and distinguishing feature of the Cotswold village and cottage. It constitutes their chief claim to rank with the best English work of any period. Other villages may show greater variety, a more individual treatment of detail and a less conservative regard for tradition, but nowhere else do the methods, the details, and the materials combine to achieve such wonderful and complete unity of expression, such abiding tranquil beauty. It is strange that in spite of their good proportions and beauty, the men who built them were occasionally careless in their construction, and ignored too

often that "the said work shall be just, true and lawful without any deceit whatsoever." There were scamps then as now, but in the main they sought perfection of workmanship, knew what was good and what was bad. Their cottages are eloquent of beautiful walls, so well built that they will probably be standing long after much present-day building.

One of the charms of the Cotswold cottages is the high-pitched roof covered with stone slates, the larger ones hung at the eaves, the sizes getting gradually smaller towards the ridge. Mr. Guy Dawber, in his notes on "Old Cottages, Farm-houses and other Stone Buildings in the Cotswold District," gives the names of these slates. He says, "The bottom or under slates at the eaves, the one bedded on the top of the walls, is called a 'cussome.' This has a slight tilt downwards, to throw the water off, and projects some 7 ins. or 8 ins. Above this the eaves commence with long and short 'eighteens,' down to long and short

BURFORD, OXFORDSHIRE

OUNDLE, NORTHAMPTONSHIRE

'elevens'; then we have long and short 'wivetts,' 'becks,' 'bachelors,' 'movedays,' 'cuttings,' and long and short 'cocks' at the apex under the cresting. They are hung dry with oak or deal pegs, which are driven tight into holes in the slates, whilst they are being sorted to sizes, or else nailed in the ordinary manner. When plastered or torched with hair mortar, level with the underside of the laths, they will last for years, as so many existing buildings testify. The 'valleys' are formed of the same slates, in a wide sweep with no hard line of demarcation where the roofs intersect, laid in regular formation and ranging with the ordinary slating. Each valley slate has its distinctive name, the centre one being the 'bottomer' with two 'lie-byes' on either side, and above and below in the next courses two 'skews' to break joint."

The cottages of Derbyshire have a distinct character of their own, although the material is the same. The stone-work is bolder and coarser in detail, the builders less playful, and the work generally much more akin to the cottages of Lancashire than of the Cotswold district. The transom in the windows is a feature which we think is not found in Oxfordshire or Gloucestershire. The Derbyshire mill at Alport (page 111), without having any particular architectural "features," is typical of the stone walling in the district; and also the pair of cottages in the same village (page 112), although they might easily be taken by the unobservant for Gloucestershire examples. Examples of the Derbyshire cottages occur at Bakewell (page 108). They are reached by steps and have the plain jambs to doors and windows with large stone quoins. There is a Gothic feeling in

105

the door head, and in the detail of the lintel over the window in the example shown ; all the stone jambs, lintels and sills are square, with neither chamfer nor moulding. Characteristic also are the piers each side of the entrance at the foot of the steps, made in one stone, with half-round tops, and the stone built in end-ways on.

A fine door at Youlgreave (page 110) shows again the coarse feeling in the huge lintel and large quoins ; the jambs of the doorway are chamfered, but the lintel is taken across square. The tablets are not so well designed as in Gloucestershire, and are much more primitive. The one at Ashford (page 160) has the initials "F.H.A." and the "1680" arranged in the simplest and most prosaic way : " F." is placed at the top, " H.A." is placed below, and the date beneath. It is not particularly happy ; nor is the one at Little Longstone, with the initials "Z.E." and the date " 1575" planned in the apex of the gable, a favourite position for them in Derbyshire. The detail of the doorway at Ashford is much like the Cotswold example at Stow-on-the-Wold, only the brackets supporting the pent are without fluting, and in the former there is a bed moulding carried round the top of the corbel or bracket.

Some of the details of kneelers are worthy of study ; those at Stanton and at Alport (page 160) are typical. All of these border on crudeness ; for instance, the peculiar way the coping is carried over the corbelling ; note, too, how deep the corbel stone is carried back into the wall. A very simple form of door-head is that at Ashford (page 160), merely a flat piece of stone carried at each end by two small projecting brackets. A curious plan for a window jamb is noticeable at Alport (page 160).

No one can visit these counties of stone architecture without being conscious of the certainty in their work, and the unhesitating use of the traditional methods of building towards the accomplishment of the final result. There are no superfluous bits of ornament, no dragging in of unnecessary moulding, and no affectation of simplicity. From the foundations to the ridge the building rises without effort, without needless divagation, each part well proportioned, each part related to the other, and the whole harmonious and complete.

In the relation of the garden to these cottages there is apparently no conscious approach to anything like deliberate

ROTHWELL, NORTHAMPTONSHIRE

106

HADDON, DERBYSHIRE
107

design, unless we except the lodge-keeper's garden at Haddon (page 107); for the rest there are certainly noticeable definite characteristics which bring them more into line with the "formal garden" than with the irresponsible vagaries of the landscape gardener. Without being limited or curtailed by the rigid and more architectural character of Haddon or Levens, the small spaces in front of the cottages are generally laid out with some regard to the house and the passer-by. At Ebrington it was noticed that a clipped tree, cut in the form of a peacock or other bird, had been planted in the corner of the garden just at the bend of the road. Happily and well placed, it gave character to the cottage and pleasure to those that passed by. It is extraordinary the number of charming effects that are realised in all these old country gardens, without overcrowding the very limited area. Nothing could have been easier than to unduly emphasize some portions at the expense of others, or to allow one part to dominate the rest. It may be, that in examples like those at Witley, in Surrey (opp. page·157), and at Goudhurst, in Kent (page 18), the blaze of colour and the want of neatness justifies itself ; but as a rule the villagers generally attempted to reduce their gardens to some sort of order. Not-

withstanding the playfulness and irregularity of many of them, the smallest show some regard for careful arrangement. Half the charm of the example at Welford-on-Avon, in Gloucestershire (page 89), is derived from the straight avenue, terminating at the far end in the arched opening, cut and shaped in the hedge. It is generally around some such simple idea as this that the garden is laid out, the degree of primness of the hedges and the flower beds depending upon the idiosyncrasies of the owner. At Byworth, in Sussex (page 29), there is another simple and effective example, with a shaped shrub at the gates and flowers blooming on the boundary wall. Cut yews on each side of the entrances are often seen, and carefully clipped privet hedges three or four feet wide. At the back of a cottage at Broadway, in Worcestershire, there is an old garden surrounded with high walls covered by fruit trees, and the middle bed crowded with hollyhocks and other old-fashioned flowers. Between the centre plot and the narrow bed next to the walls is the pathway paved with stone flags.

BAKEWELL, DERBYSHIRE

108

BAKEWELL, DERBYSHIRE

109

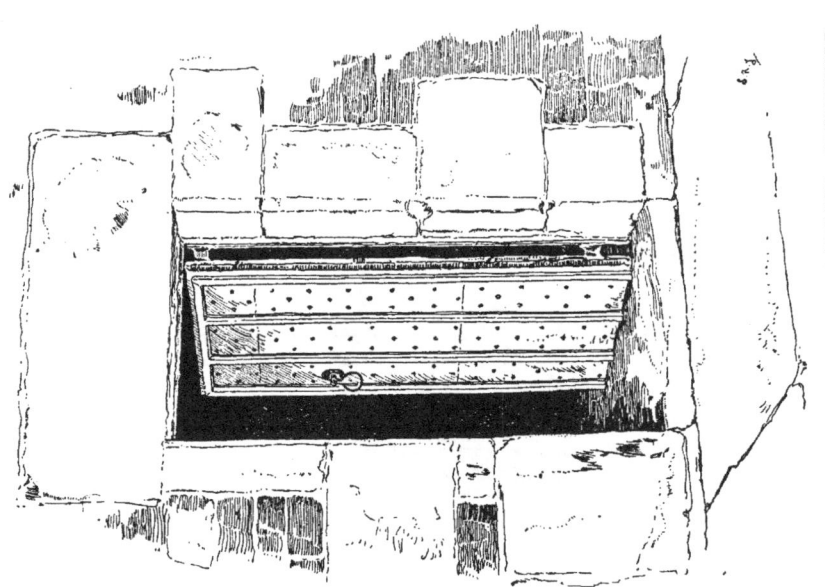

ALPORT, DERBYSHIRE

YOULGREAVE, DERBYSHIRE

ALPORT, DERBYSHIRE

111

TADDINGTON, DERBYSHIRE

113

SUCKLEY, WORCESTERSHIRE. FROM A WATER-COLOUR DRAWING BY E. A. CHADWICK.

WORCEST R

DIVISION V.

WORCESTERSHIRE, WARWICKSHIRE

V.—WORCESTERSHIRE AND WARWICKSHIRE

SLOW journey of many stops taken through Cheshire and Shropshire, across the top of Worcestershire and Warwickshire from west to east, and then southward towards the north of Gloucestershire, shows within a small area and with certain limitations the gradual changes which took place in the development of the ancient cottage. To the first stage belong those of wood and plaster, to the second those of timber and brick, to the third those of brick, and then finally those of stone. These changes, it need hardly be said, did not follow nor necessarily grow out of each other, like all consistent and respectable traditions have a way of doing, but jumped forward and backward in each county in the most wayward and irresponsible fashion ; and in this respect the cottages of Warwickshire and Worcestershire were no exception. The majority of them are of brick and timber, with many later examples of brick that retain the same proportions and some of the peculiarities of the earlier buildings. In no detail is this so apparent as in the dormer and the unbroken frieze between the top of the ground-floor windows and the underside of the eaves. The frieze runs

BROADWAY, WORCESTERSHIRE

from end to end of one or a number of cottages, and is as characteristic as the dormer, and the frequent raising of the ground-floor three and four steps above the road. In the cottages at Chaddesley Corbett, in Worcestershire (below), the effect of this deep frieze is partly lost owing to the vertical and sloping half-timber work, but directly the brick and timber is translated into brick the frieze effect becomes emphasised, as at Ludington, in Warwickshire (page 131). These are practically the cottages in the foreground at Knowle (page 136) turned into brick with the same proportions, only the roof and dormers are covered with thatch instead of tiles. At Solihull there are a number of them which follow still more closely the characteristics of the half-timber cottage, these having actually the same number of steps up to the front doors.

Where they differ is in the glazing of the windows and the frame, which is set back an inch, instead of being flush, as in the early cottage; and in the use of brick walls instead of timber framing and brick panels. The dormer not only persists in the brick, but in the stone district as well, both in the older stone-mullioned type and the Georgian examples, as for instance at Broadway, in Worcestershire (page 119), and many of those at Mickleton, in Gloucestershire. This resemblance is perhaps all the more remarkable as both the materials and the methods of construction are dissimilar. In the south-eastern counties and those of Cheshire, Shropshire and Herefordshire, where the methods are much the same, there are only a few examples of dormers which in any way resemble them. Most of these are gabled, a few hipped, and others are

CHADDESLEY CORBETT, WORCESTERSHIRE

BROADWAY, WORCESTERSHIRE

covered by part of the main roof, which is carried over the window at a flatter pitch, as at Shottery (page 139) and Pershore (opposite).

Although these are some of the chief points which distinguish these cottages from those of other counties where the same materials were used, there is altogether a less careful consideration of external detail and a greater tendency to repeat in one village what has been done in another. The chimneys, for instance, are nearly all finished with one or two projecting courses and one above set flush with the brickwork below. Occasionally the stacks are placed angle-wise on the plan, as in the cottages at Chaddesley Corbett (page 118), in Worcestershire, and at Hampton Lucy, in Warwickshire (page 138); but these are exceptions, for generally there is neither the same fancy, skill, nor careful consideration of those little points of detail which add to the charm of the cottages in Kent. The middle cottage at Shottery, in Warwickshire (page 139), shows an attempt to do without a gutter next to the chimney by continuing the roof above the ridge till it meets the stack; but this is obviously an afterthought, and not a very happy one; and then again, with one or two exceptions, such as the example at Charlecote, in Warwickshire (page 135), no attempt is made to connect the chimney flanking the side walls with the main roof, a detail that is solved satisfactorily over and over again in Surrey. The projecting stepped brickwork, occasionally used for the drip of the chimney, above the tile roof, is similar to that already noted at Alderley Edge, in Cheshire (page 65); but in this district it is more often made to fulfil the purpose of a verge in the later cottages. When used in this position the little triangular spaces left on the upper edge are filled in with mortar, the roofing tiles being laid direct upon it. This same

BROADWAY, WORCESTERSHIRE

120

PERSHORE, WORCESTERSHIRE. FROM A WATER-COLOUR DRAWING BY WILMOT PILSBURY.

covered by part of the main roof, which is carried over the window at a flatter pitch, as at Shottery (page 191) and Pershore (opposite).

Although these are some of the chief points which distinguish these cottages from those of other counties where the same materials were used, there is altogether a less careful consideration of external detail and a greater tendency to repeat in one village what has been done in another. The chimneys, for instance, are nearly all finished with one or two projecting courses and one above set flush with the brickwork below. Occasionally the stacks are placed angle-wise on the plan, as in the cottages at Chaddesley Corbett (page 118), in Worcestershire, and at Hampton Lucy, in Warwickshire (page 138); but these are exceptions, for generally there is neither the same fancy, skill, nor consideration of those little points of detail which add to the charm

. . . Kent. The middle cottage at Shottery, in Warwickshire . . . an attempt to do without a gutter next to the chimney . . . above the ridge till it meets the stack; but this is . . . a very happy one; and then again, with . . . the example at Charlecote, in Warwick-

shire (page 139) no attempt is made to connect the chim-ney flanking the side walls with the main roof, a detail that is . . .

. . . . for the purpose of a verge in the later cottages. When used in this position the little triangular spaces left on the upper edge are filled in with mortar, the roofing slate being laid direct . . . . This same . . .

BROADWAY, WORCESTERSHIRE

PERSHORE, WORCESTERSHIRE. FROM A WATER-COLOUR DRAWING BY WILMOT PILSBURY, R.W.S.

method of using brick has been noticed in the finish of a brick label. An unusual use of brick, perhaps too ingenious to be ancient, was noticed at Bromsgrove, near Birmingham. The bricks are laid with the width as face work, one course of stretchers alternating with another of one stretcher, and two headers, one on each side and placed on end; by this wonderful arrangement the headers are left projecting beyond the face of the shaft in every other course. The pigeon-holes which have been noticed in the cottages and farmhouses of the Cotswold are carried out here in brick on similar lines, a course of headers taking the place of the stone bands, and the openings cut in the four courses of brick between those that project. The base for the framing is set up on stone (page 134) or brick. Mill Street, Warwick (page 129), has both. The wood sill of the half timbers, which in Cheshire is almost invariably set back from the masonry, is flush with the base, and the uprights recessed instead. These uprights, in the dwellings halfway up the street, average 7 ins., the spaces between 10 ins., and are filled in with brick. The brick-

work throughout these counties is usually laid Flemish bond, four courses to 11 ins., and with wide joints. At Hampton Lucy, in Warwickshire (page 138), there is an exceptional brick cottage covered with thatch, the others in the village being half timber and brick, and brick with the usual characteristics of frieze and dormer. Custom, tradition, and especially material, rooted to the soil the various types of cottage building, but in the metal work of the villages there are characteristics more obviously common to all. For instance, a Worcestershire or Warwickshire fire-dog was not

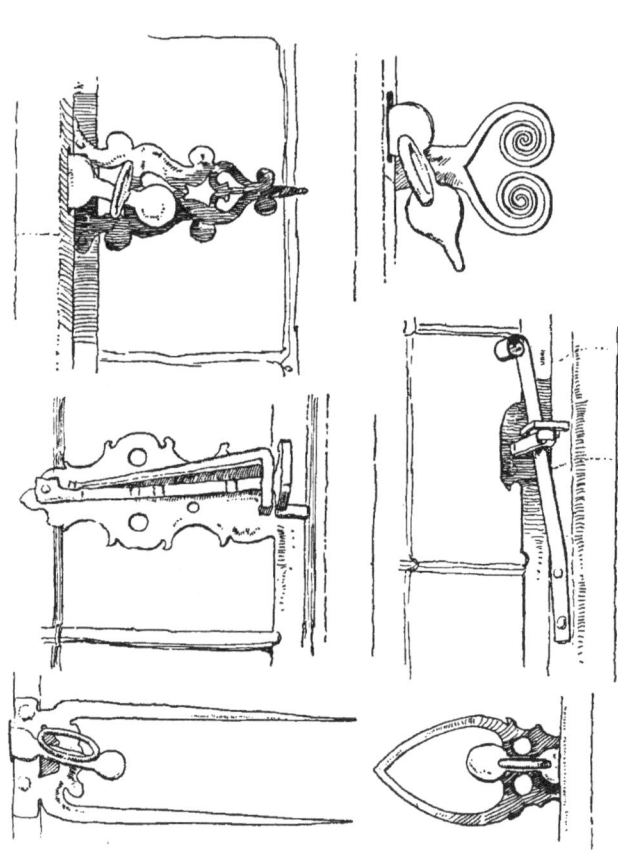

CASEMENT FITTINGS

RIPPLE, WORCESTERSHIRE.

necessarily so different from a Gloucestershire example, for the material and the purpose would be the same, while in the cottages of the same districts neither the methods of construction nor the materials were alike. Much more depended upon individual fancy and workmanship. Windows in the stone counties repeat time after time, but the window fasteners are seldom the same. The great charm about this work lies in its unconscious regard for essentials ; for instance, there is not much that can be said for the pot cranes beyond the fact that they supplied a need in the most economical and straightforward way. All that was required was an upright, an arm and its support, and that was what the smith gave his customer, adding a little incidental decoration by the way. In one instance the end is turned and finished with a scroll, in another the support for the arm is considered, while in a third the end of the arm is beaten into a leaf. None of this is very great art, perhaps, but sufficient to raise it from the commonplace; just that labour and cunning which separate the good from the cheap. The notion that good work, good proportions and intelligent arrangement of parts are as cheap as badly executed or badly

planned work, is the result of ignorance. This old metal work, no less than the cottages in which it is found, is the outcome of long service and association with materials, of innumerable failures and successes, and of a constant if varying desire to produce what is good and beautiful. It is never cheap nor hurried, but has the stamp of leisurely production. That the makers were proud of their work is often reflected in it ; names occasionally occur, on the pieces, and the finish and execution leave little to be desired. Ironwork was occasionally introduced as a support for the pents. Brackets of scroll work occur at Belbroughton, in Worcestershire, and less elaborate ones can be seen at Welford-on-Avon, in Gloucestershire (page 162) ; garden gates were also carried out in wrought iron. There is

YARDLEY WOOD, WORCESTERSHIRE

124

a simple and effective treatment at Binton, in Warwickshire (page 167), and although one questions the wisdom of stopping the uprights below the top bar, the effect is light and appropriate. Another more satisfactory and elaborate piece of work is the window balcony at Henley-in-Arden, in Warwickshire (page 167), unfortunately mutilated, but with sufficient remaining to give an idea of what it was like in its complete condition. The scroll work is welded to the uprights at three points in the height, and the middle piece above the bar leans forward, supported by a stay from the upright. The cast and wrought-iron knockers, the lock plates, latches and handles, are all of interesting detail, and range from the severe circular cast brass knocker to the florid wrought example.

Other interesting pierced and cut work is noticeable among the lock plates (page 166), and the footman in bright iron at Welford-on-Avon, in Gloucestershire, is a splendid example of wrought, hammered and pierced work of interlacing pattern and of simple construction (page 161). Of this simplicity the village smith may have been in ignorance, for it is probable that if he could have engraved on the pieces, cast portions of them, or had thoughts of combining these methods to make them more elaborate, he would have done so to the best of his ability and as far as his knowledge carried him, like he did in the rest of his work. That was *his* simplicity, and quite a different thing to the affectation of it that is so detestable in much modern work. The latches, handles and casement fasteners (pages 58 and 159), are of the kind that we should expect to find in a cottage ; but many of the others are remarkable for their exceptional refinement. The scroll-work, for example, on one of the fasteners illustrated on page 122 is of dainty and delicate workmanship, and would be as much in harmony with the interior of a mansion as of a cottage. The same characteristic is noticeable in the footman (page 161), the metal work

ATCH LENCH, WORCESTERSHIRE

126

CLEEVE PRIOR, WORCESTERSHIRE

127

at Weston-Patrick (page 43), to which we have already referred, the soft modelling of the cast-iron fire-dogs and firebacks in Sussex (page 163), and the examples at Chiddingfold, in Surrey, and Sandhurst Green, in Kent (page 161). The half timber might be casual and the brickwork poor, but the metal work here, as elsewhere, was generally up to a high standard of workmanship and in advance of the other trades, with the exception, perhaps, of the Cotswold district, which seems to have developed more or less on the same level. The other trades might be wanting, but the smith could always be relied on to supply fine and interesting work.

Between the forged gates next to the roadway and the cast brass knocker on the cottage door was the garden, "the betweenity," as the late J. D. Sedding called it—a link to connect the dwelling with its natural surroundings, a small space, but arranged as carefully by the order-loving owner as the "formal garden" of the large manor-house ; for whatever may be the merits of the landscape system, there can be no question that the charm of the old cottage garden lies in its order, neatness, and making the most of the small area. There was no room either for pergolas, bridges, sun-dials, summer-houses and broad terraces. These were for the squire at the manor-house ; but in the design of the approach, the fencing, the walls, the gates, the planning of the old-fashioned flower-beds, the cutting of the occasional clipped trees and hedges, and the arch over the entrance, the cottager found ample scope for his fancy. If the cottages were close on the road, without front gardens, some natural beauty near at hand was shaped and fashioned, brought to order, and made part of the village. It might be a clump of trees, a pond, as at Upton Grey, Hampshire (page 40), or the village green with the road on each side. Here might be the village cross or the village pump ; round the trees, seats, and the pond emphasized with posts and guard

WARWICK

128

rails. One of the characteristics of the old cottage garden is the division which cuts it off from the roadway and its neighbours. It cannot be said that every district had its own type of garden, but many of the details have their local peculiarities. The cottage at Hill Wootton, in Warwickshire (pages 132 and 133), shows a type of division common enough in a great many parts of the county. The palings are nailed to two rails, one at the top and one at the bottom, these being generally housed or tenoned into the posts, placed at regular intervals from 9 ft. to 10 ft. apart. The tops of the uprights are either square or shaped. A more interesting example is the fence common in Kent and Surrey. The posts are about the same distance apart, and of sufficient depth from front to back to take the rails and boarding, and to allow for a projection on the outer face. The rails, three in number and of triangular section, are placed one just below the top of the fence, another about 9 ins. below, and the third kept well above the ground. They are tenoned and pinned into the posts, and the boards are wedge-shaped, each set a little behind the other; they are then nailed to the rails, the nails taking a zigzag pattern. The boards vary from $2\frac{1}{2}$ to 4 ins. wide. At Blythburgh, in Suffolk, the same fencing has been used, with the boarding reversed at every post. There are other varieties of the fence, but this is the method generally adopted. Wattled fencing is found occasionally in Gloucestershire, and a thatched example was noticed at Filby Broad, in Norfolk. Dry stone walls are usual in the Cotswold, and in Devon slaty stone walls, whitewashed, are general. The garden walls in Norfolk and Suffolk are often flint, with brick copings and bases, and brick dressings next to the gateways. Another form of garden fence is similar to the partial filling in of the porch at

HAMPTON-IN-ARDEN, WARWICKSHIRE

130

LUDINGTON, WARWICKSHIRE

131

LEEK WOOTTON, WARWICKSHIRE

HILL WOOTTON, WARWICKSHIRE

132

LEEK WOOTTON, WARWICKSHIRE

134

SOLIHULL, WARWICKSHIRE

Atch Lench in Worcestershire (page 126) : an example occurs also at Milton Bryant, in Bedfordshire (page 168). At Cranbrook, in Kent (page 14), the fence is of four rails between pairs of posts set some distance apart and filled in with cross-pieces that leave openings of diamond shapes. In addition to these are the clipped hedges of hawthorn and holly.

Some of the yew trees at the entrances to the gardens, or that form avenues, like those at Cleeve Prior, Worcestershire (page 127), are cut into all manner of wonderful and fascinating shapes. At Cleeve Prior are to be seen, hand in hand, "the glorious company of Apostles," and the Evangelists, memoralised in the form of sixteen yews. Those at Broadway, Worcestershire (page 120), are of the simpler variety ; more elaborate examples are found at Yardley Wood (page 124), where the lower part of the trees is arched over the entrance and the tops shaped like cones. The "pleaching," or cutting and trimming of the trees at Lapworth, Warwickshire (page 140), is remarkably fine. At Solihull, Warwickshire (above), there is a single yew tree, the lower part cut away on one side to form an arbour, and on the top is perched a bird. Another example at Risley Hall, Derbyshire, is in the form of two doves ; and there are other interesting trees at Ripple,

CHARLECOTE, WARWICKSHIRE

Worcestershire (page 123). It is these flights of fancy and imagination, in the hedges and trees of the gardens they adorned, that formed the link between the dwelling and the world of nature ; for while there is underlying all the same natural love of order and beauty that we find in the cottage, it is more freely expressed, and less hampered by the restrictions of the builder and craftsman. One of the most charming and engaging descriptions of the old garden was written by William Lawson early in the seventeenth century. He says, " What can your eye desire to see, your care to heare, your mouth to taste, or your nose to smell that is not to be had in an orchard with abundance and beauty ? What more delightsome than an infinite varietie of sweet smelling flowers ? decking with sundrye colours the greene mantel of the earth, the universal mother of us all, so by them bespotted, so dyed, that all the world cannot sample them, and wherein it is more fit to admire the Dyer than imitate his workmanship, colouring not only the earth but decking the ayre, and sweetening every breath and spirit. The rose red, damaske, velvet, and double double province rose, the sweet muske rose double and single, the double and single white rose, the faire and sweet scenting woodbind double and single ; Purple cowslips and double cowslips, primrose double and single, the violet nothing behind the best for smelling sweetly, and a thousand more will provoke your contente, and all these by the skill of your Gardener so comely and orderly placed in your Borders and squares." [1]

[1] Quoted from " The Formal Garden in England," by Reginald Blomfield and F. Inigo Thomas.

KNOWLE, WARWICKSHIRE

ALVESTON, WARWICKSHIRE

137

HAMPTON LUCY, WARWICKSHIRE
138

SHOTTERY, WARWICKSHIRE

139

LAPWORTH, WARWICKSHIRE
140

LUSTLEIGH, DEVONSHIRE. FROM AN OIL-PAINTING BY GROSVENOR THOMAS.

DEVONSOM

DIVISION VI.

DEVONSHIRE, WEST SOMERSETSHIRE

VI.—DEVONSHIRE AND WEST SOMERSETSHIRE.

DEVONSHIRE is the most beautiful county in England, and shares with West Somersetshire the distinction of a cottage tradition more rural than that of any other. Homely, comfortable, and hospitable-looking are the best terms to describe these cottages. Architecturally interesting they would hardly be called by the unsympathetic stranger, but to the thorough-going born-and-bred countryman of these counties, who never —if he can help it—takes five minutes to do a thing when ten will do equally well, these old places are the best and most beautiful in the world. As simple and homely as the "gert Jan Ridd," they are the work of men such as he, who thought, laboured, and lived in a leisurely fashion as only the true native could and does do to this very day. This cottage-building tradition seems to be as extinct as that creature the "dodo," although the villager still holds to the ancient ways of his forefathers of spending twice as long over a job as any other known workman and charging half as much. Here, at least, is the spirit of the old builders that gave much and asked little— that gave us the buttressed, plastered, and whitewashed cob walls, the big square chimneys, and the somewhat casually-thatched roofs of the Devonshire and Somersetshire cottages. There is not one built severely square, and but few have a complete gable or hip. They follow the contours of

DAWLISH, DEVONSHIRE

143

DAWLISH, DEVONSHIRE

144

DAWLISH   DEVONSHIRE

LANDEWEDNACK, CORNWALL. FROM A WATER-COLOUR
DRAWING BY MRS. E. STANHOPE FORBES, A.R.W.S.

THURLESTONE, DEVONSHIRE

the ground haphazard—picturesque and rambling, like the talk of a native, they are as pleasant to look at as the other is to listen to. The walls never seem upright, the windows appear to be placed anywhere, and the thatch does not cover the roof so carefully and neatly as it might do. Casual and careless, with many faults, and no finish, might fairly be the description given to them by a foreigner. Every part seems wanting, but the whole has that indefinable charm that probably springs from their relationship to the surroundings. Of these cottages it can truly be said that they are growths of the soil, trimmed and clipped somewhat by man, but never enough that they can be described as " works of art." There is a little design perhaps, some putting together of mud material, some thatch, and that is the cottage ; but the rest somehow escapes us, for one finds the trees, the hedgerows, the orchards, the sun, the rain, and the rocks have a real and intimate part in the result, as will be seen in the illustrations on pages 147 and 150, and opposite page 141.

In some villages the cob walls have been built direct on the rock, after the side has been roughly hewn to a vertical or slightly battering

NORTON FITZWARREN, SOMERSET

face, and the top made level for the cob. When of a rocky character this natural foundation seems to have taken the place of the usual base of stone or brick. Upon it was built the cob wall in layers of about 18 ins. of mud, gravel, or small gritty stone, trodden down by the feet, and battered with a wooden beater. A wisp of straw was carried by the workman under his arm, who, as needed, strewed it beneath his feet. After the wall was up the surface was chopped down, faced with plaster, and then white-washed. The base was generally tarred, as in the cottages at Dawlish, in Devonshire (page 143), and at Minehead and Dulverton, in Somer-setshire (pages 149 and 153). In the fence or boundaries the walls were sometimes left without plaster.

In parts of Somerset the cottages are built of a pinky stone of roughly coursed masonry, and at Crowcombe some of the boundary walls are of random rubble, the cavities and joints of which are plastered with mortar, and a jointer or similar tool drawn across the face of it. When the walls are built of stone they are generally about 18 ins. thick, with the external

146

SELWORTHY, SOMERSETSHIRE

147

and internal coats of plaster in addition. Cob walls are 2 ft. thick, more or less. In the case of a big door or gateway being introduced, the angles are protected with masonry tailing into the cob work, and for the same reason the corners of dwellings and of windows are rounded in many instances. The windows are small and set back from the face of the wall, the angles rounded or occasionally, as at Crowcombe, the plaster is finished with a smooth face for the width of 4 or 5 ins. round the openings, which, without exactly being an architrave, gives the suggestion of one.

The buttresses, generally of stone, introduced to strengthen the walls, are a characteristic feature and frequently of enormous size, the projection at the base measuring as much as 2 ft. 6 ins., the width 3 ft., and diminishing from the bottom to the top in one long slope (page 143). They are generally placed either at the ends or at certain points along the front, and frequently in a line with the chimney stack, rising from the ridge. Most of them are built of slatey stone whitewashed and without any coat of plaster. When the angles of the cottage are not strengthened by these buttresses they are rounded, and where the walls are of the common slatey stone and finished with plaster, the corners are still rounded, probably copied from the cob walling. The chimneys are of the same stone and carried well up above the eaves, and then completed with a projecting course of slate (page 153), and in some cases with about 9 ins. of similar rough masonry inclining inwards like the slope of a buttress. Others are taken up in stone sufficiently high to clear the eaves of the roof, with the upper part in brick, as, for example, at Minehead in Somersetshire (pages 149 and 150), and at Thurlestone in South Devon (page 145). The village of Braunton, in North Devon, has a number of these sturdy chimney stacks with brick tops, that look

148

MINEHEAD, SOMERSETSHIRE

MINEHEAD, SOMERSETSHIRE

150

like later additions, the height of the brickwork in many cases not being more than 18 ins. to 2 ft. The chimneys that flank the fronts of the dwellings almost invariably project considerably into the roadway or garden, and the slopes, which diminish its bulk towards the top, are either covered with slates or pantiles, as in the cottage at Minehead (page 150), and also in the one at Dawlish (page 144). The diversity in the number and direction of these slopes is remarkable, and gives considerable character to this striking feature of the cottage. Another variety of chimney top to that which has already been described is also depicted in the cottage illustrated on page 150. Four small brick piers are placed parallel to the faces of the masonry, or in some cases angle-wise; these support a thin stone slab, leaving an opening on each side. A drip of slate is built into the walls following the line of the roof in a series of steps where the chimney appears through the thatch.

The boundary walls of stone are sometimes coped with slate and sloped inward from each side of the wall. The dry walls, more often used for ditching than the fences between gardens, are laid in courses of the usual slatey

material, one course sloped in one direction, and the next in the reverse. In looking along these courses of stone the effect is one of light and shade, grey and bluish-grey bands that rise and fall at every change in the level of the ground.

Thatching was the common method of roofing in the counties of Devonshire and Somersetshire, but like the building of cob walls, it has gradually fallen into disrepute except for a little patching and the occasional covering of an old dwelling. This is partly the result of enforcing unsuitable bye-laws upon the rural districts, and the extra expense entailed in keeping it in good order and repair. The short-sighted desire for cheap labourers' cottages, and the additional trouble of looking after this form of roof are also amongst some of the other reasons for its almost complete disuse in this country. In Kent and Sussex, and two or three other districts, there has lately been some attempt to

SELWORTHY, SOMERSETSHIRE

151

carry on the traditions of the beautiful craft of thatching, but the tendency of local authorities is to discourage its use. The number of thatched cottages of considerable age which have survived the risks of fire, would probably astonish these unenlightened authorities. Not only is it in Devonshire and Somersetshire that the use of thatch has been so general, but there are beautiful examples to be found in nearly every district throughout England, indeed it would be difficult to improve upon some in Sussex, Gloucestershire and Oxfordshire (opp. pages 83, 98 and 102). A particularly fine example was noticed just outside Mayfield. The hazel rods, used for the purpose of keeping the thatch in place, were laid over the ridge, the hips and the eaves crossing and recrossing one another, and caught under the loops of the pegging pieces at the intersections. In Suffolk and Norfolk, Berkshire and Hampshire, and in all the wood and timber counties, numbers of thatches are to be seen ; and in the stone district the thatching is neat and worked round the windows and dormers in the most delightful manner. In Somersetshire very few hazel rods are used at the ridge and the eaves, while in Devonshire the thatcher did not appear to trouble much how his thatching was finished. It is neither so carefully nor so completely executed as in other counties. A peculiarity of the method in Somersetshire was to bring the thatch to a point at the end of the ridge above the line of hazel rods, that are laid along the thatch just beneath the cresting.

At the village of Williton, in Somersetshire (page 155), there are some fine examples of hipped thatched dormers, with the cocked-out ridge, and a suggestion of the double cresting along the main roof, so characteristic of the barns in Norfolk and Suffolk. Ridges have been noticed in Devonshire

CROWCOMBE, SOMERSETSHIRE

152

finished with single hazel rods bent to the form of a triangle, the points of the bases touching—a feature that has been copied by the brickmakers in the district as a pattern for their tile ridging. In the one case it looks rather well, in the other hideous.

The old name for a thatcher was " helyer," and long after slating had to some extent taken the place of thatch, the slater was known by that name, the slates being called " helying stones." In North Devon small grey slates of a pleasant colour were frequently used on the projecting portions that stopped at the first-floor level. Walled-in and open porches, small bays and ovens, and similar parts were nearly always roofed in this way when the rest of the covering was of thatch. Some of the roofs in the small towns have similar slate roofs ; and at the seaside village of Morthoe the sides of the chimneys of a farmhouse were hung with them, diamond shapes being introduced into the plain slate hanging. Examples of the small roofs occur at Braunton, Dawlish and Thurlestone (pages 143, 144 and 145). In many of the villages the narrow side-walks and the garden paths are laid with small pebbles at right angles to the curb, in some simple pattern that suggests strips, obtained by alternating rows of thin pebbles with thick ones, and occasionally rising to the dignity of a diamond-shape in a different coloured pebble.

If we would have again the varied details and homely beauty of the old cottage in Devonshire and elsewhere, there must grow up a living tradition, based on a knowledge of the original work, to replace our ideal of " cheapness." To make the cheap production of things the criterion by which they are to be judged means poor work, inefficient craftsmen, and the ultimate degradation of our surroundings. We must revive the old-fashioned belief in perfection of workmanship, use, and beauty. Then, and only then, will play the fountains of invention and beauty in every village and hamlet up and down the countryside.

154

COMBE FLOREY, SOMERSETSHIRE

NORTON FITZWARREN, SOMERSETSHIRE

156

A COTTAGE GARDEN. FROM A WATER-COLOUR DRAWING BY MISS ROSA WALLIS.

(By Permission of R. L. Gunther, Esq.)

CONCLUSION.

A COTTAGE GARDEN. FROM A WATER-COLOUR DRAWING BY MISS ROSA WAL

CONCLUSION.

CONCLUSION.

VERY visitor to an English village appreciates the picturesqueness of the old cottage, and everyone can enjoy what has been so well called " the artless inadvertences, the casual patchwork of the old walls, the overlapping of successive developments, the unsophisticated craft of it," and all those incidental beauties that have grown since the day of completion, when Time began to colour the walls and roofs in his own fashion ; and successive generations patched and repatched, and added a portion here and a portion there to the original structure. As a rule the admiration goes no further, and the visitor leaves the scene with a more or less confused notion of gables, dormers, roofs and chimneys, covered with vegetation, that he remembers vaguely long after and sufficiently well to describe as " picturesque." As far as it goes this may do well enough, but unfortunately out of this nebulous impression there has grown the idea that the old country cottage is a haphazard arrangement of one or two rooms pitchforked together anyhow, and developed in a happy-go-lucky fashion into the picturesque object, the old English cottage. In only a modified sense is this true, for however much the cottage was added to, altered or patched, the simple oblong plan and elevation of four walls remained the backbone of its beauty. It might be lengthened, and the width increased by one or even two aisles; bays and porches, too, might be added, but the central form, definite and unmistakable, always dominated. Directly this was lost sight of and the original purpose ignored or forgotten, the additions and " picturesqueness " became meaningless. In all the finest examples, whether many gabled as those in the Cotswold, or roofed like those in Kent, the persistence of the main lines of

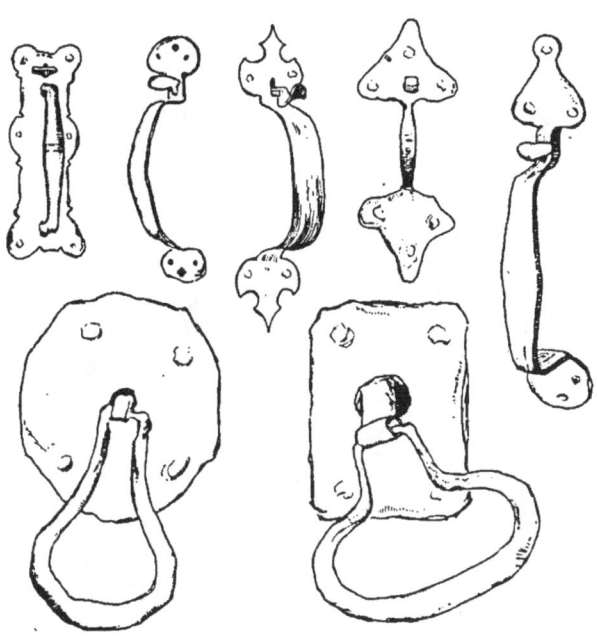

IRON DOOR LATCHES AND HANDLES

159

the plan in the expression of the exterior controls and gives significance to all the rest.

With so many materials and such a variety of methods in use, one is apt to over-estimate the "picturesque" and to under-value the less obvious but more important qualities of order and balance. And yet there can be no question that the latter were always at the back of the builder's mind. Behind individuality, local peculiarities, the unusual and spontaneous, these were unceasingly at work. Out of this sprang their originality and freshness. New ways were but the improving, ordering, and more effective arrangement of the old. Variety with them meant steps towards the final and perfect arrangement, and change for its own sake was

an "originality" of which they were probably never guilty. The additional course of bricks in the Kent chimney, the modification of a stone mullion in the Cotswold windows, or the invention of a new frill for the edging of a thatch roof in a Norfolk village, were changes made for improvement's sake. The feverish anxiety to be new and different never entered the slow and leisurely minds of the villagers; and so slow were they to change that they clung to old methods when new ones with advantage could have been adopted; but transitions from one material to another often came too quickly for the builder to accommodate himself at once to the peculiarities of a new

DETAILS OF STONEWORK

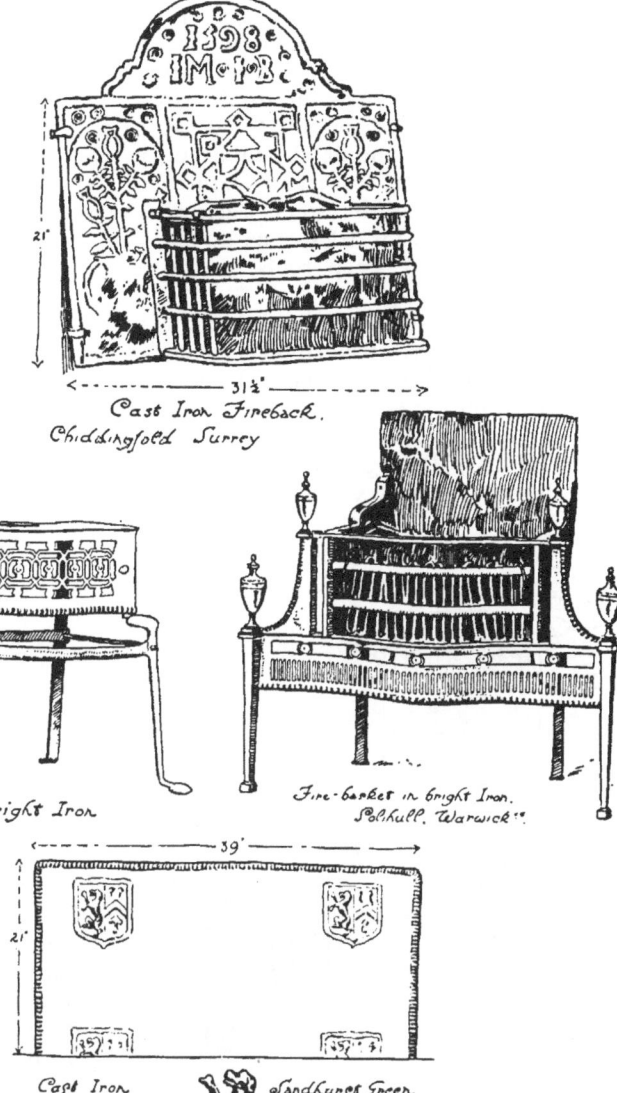

Cast Iron Fireback.
Chiddingfold Surrey

Footman in bright Iron.
Welford on Avon,
Glos

Fire-basket in bright Iron.
Solihull, Warwick[re]

Cast Iron   Sandhurst Green.
Fireback.   Kent.

Detail on Shield

FIREPLACE ACCESSORIES

161

material. Some of these changes have been noticed already in preceding chapters : Sussex, for instance, where the old ways of working a material were still retained when the material itself was different. Warwickshire and Gloucestershire showed a similar although not so marked a change, as certain features were as suitable for the stone slates of Gloucestershire as for tiles, such as the gable dormers and steep roofs of the Warwickshire cottage.

Another change occurs in passing from the east to the west of Norfolk. Instead of the brick and flint, the materials commonly used on the east coast, stone with galleted joints became of frequent occurrence. This galleting is unlike that in Kent, Surrey or Sussex. The joints of

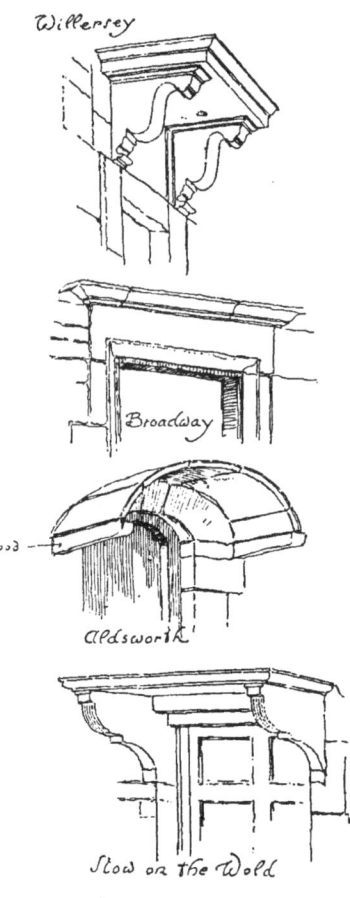

DOORHEADS

162

the masonry are as wide as in Kent, but the small stones are placed on the flat and a little distance apart.

It is to be observed that while the characteristic uses of a local material enable us to discriminate between one neighbourhood and another, it would be a mistake, as we have seen throughout the foregoing pages, to assume an entirely consistent development of cottage architecture in one district. A village

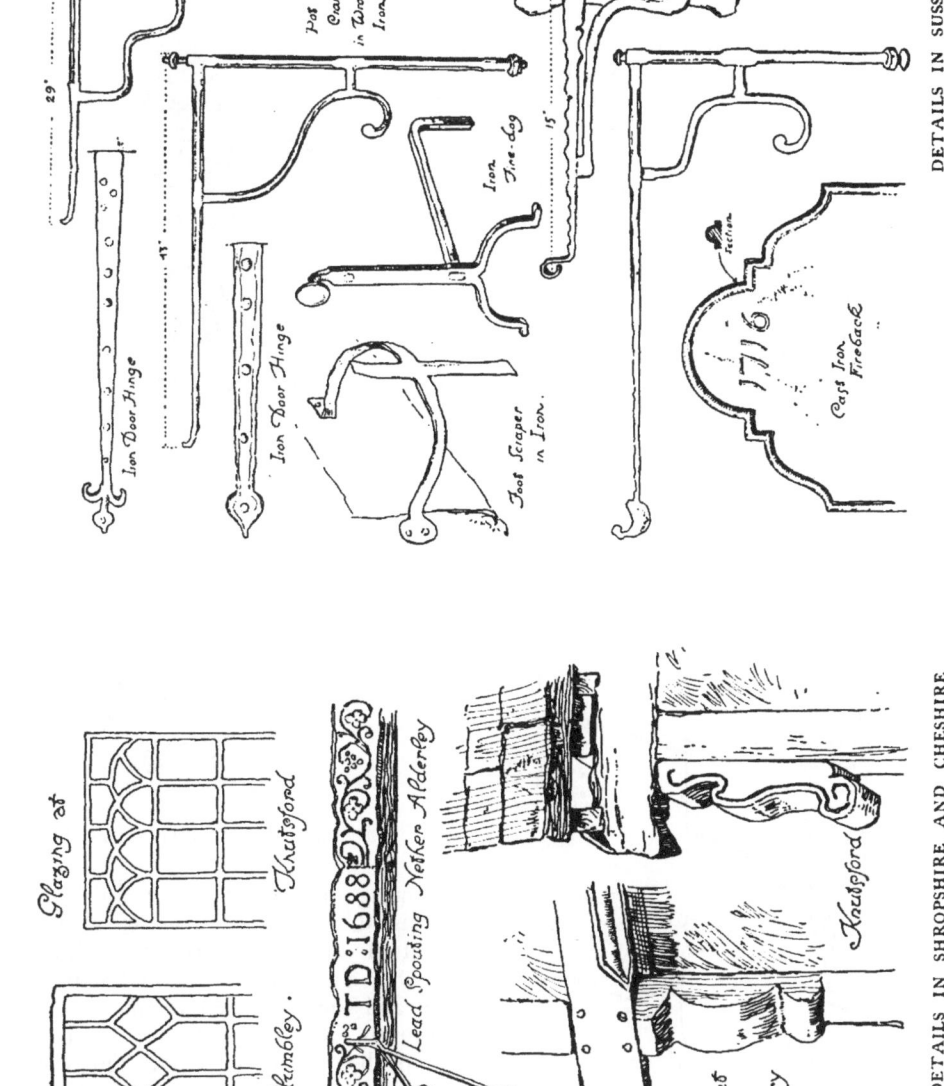

DETAILS IN SUSSEX

Pot Cranes in Wrought Iron

Iron Fire-Dog

Iron Door Hinge

Iron Door Hinge

Foot Scraper in Iron.

Cast Iron FireBack

DETAILS IN SHROPSHIRE AND CHESHIRE

Glazing at

Knutsford

Plumbley.

TD·1688

Lead Spouting Nether Alderley

Knutsford

Bracket at Onibury

163

may have some peculiarly local detail, as for example at Stanway, where the thatched roofs are finished at the ridge by a twisting of the thatch into a rope pattern ; or the exceptional walling that has been noticed at Middleton ; or again the elaborate fixing of the thatch roof on a cottage near Wellington, in Shropshire. Even the brick barns vary in the honeycombing of the walls for ventilation. In Worcestershire the perforations are in long parallel lines ; in Cheshire and Shropshire they are arranged in the form of diamonds and half diamonds, with the points towards each other, while in Norfolk they are in alternate courses of one and two openings. Another particularly local variation has been noted in the wood and timber district, where the panels between the wood

WATCHET, SOMERSETSHIRE

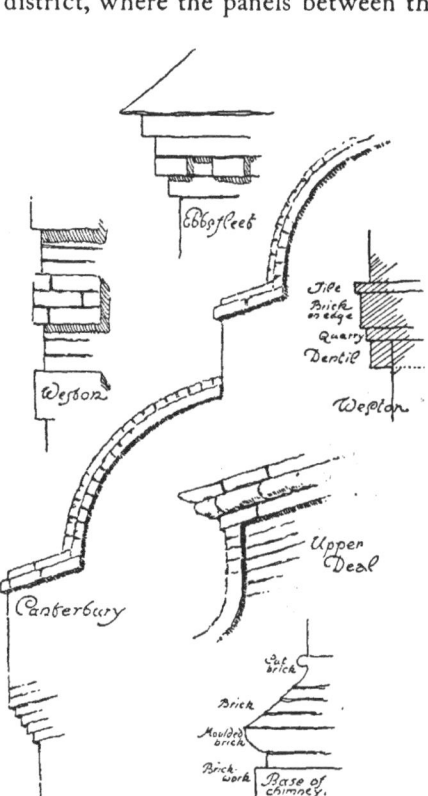

ARCHITECTURAL DETAILS

164

framing, instead of being finished, as usual, with a coat of plaster richly matted with hair, have been filled in with a mixture of crushed alabaster and lime, finished to an almost smooth face, the alabaster coming from the quarries near by. This use of an unusual material or method, or the alteration of a traditional form, did not mean that the builders dropped the old way for the new; the introduction of hipped roofs, for instance, was not the beginning of the end for the gable. Indeed, nothing is more remarkable than its persistence from the earliest to the latest examples of the old cottage. With the exception of the county of Kent the gable predominates everywhere, the half-gable and half-hipped and the wholly-hipped roof being rare in comparison with the other form. The steep pitch of many of the pantile roofs in Norfolk and Suffolk is probably the continuance of the same form when thatch was the common roofing material ; the same steep pitch is noticeable in the Cotswolds and in the Midlands. One might say of these cottages that changes were so slow that they always appeared the same to the villager ; decade followed decade with few alterations, and outside influences only touched remotely the newly-built cottages that were added along the sides of the street. And the past was always with them ; never a new building that had not something

Stanton

Stanton

Colne Roger

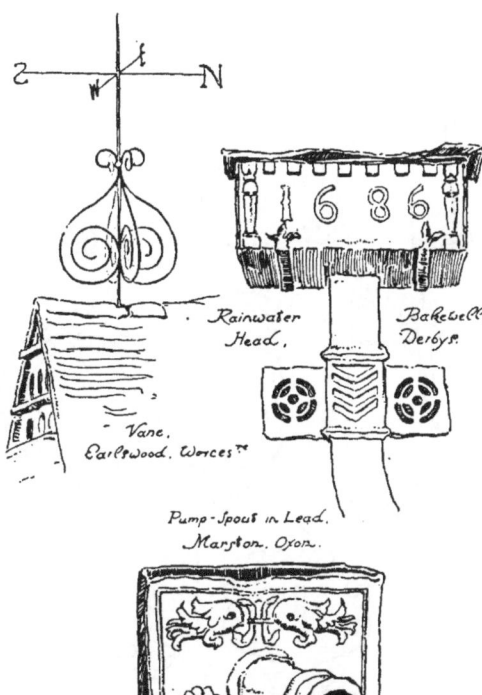

DETAILS OF EXTERIOR DECORATION

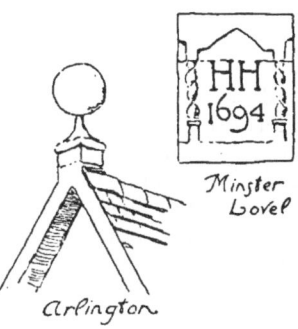

Minster Lovel

Arlington

DETAILS OF STONEWORK

of the old, never a detail that was not related to one already in the cottage next door ; and every Sunday, as the villager went down or up the road to the church, he saw very much what he had always seen. In the background of the village stood the church, the pivot upon which the whole village life revolved. The inn was on one side of the church, and on the other abutted the cottages of the village, tailing

165

away down the street. The church and the cottages grouped round about it are frequently the most beautiful part of the village. They form, too, the last bulwark against the cheap and pernicious influence of modern town life and its uninteresting methods of building. The further away from the church and the nearer to the outskirts of the village the more obvious becomes the encroachment of the cheap cottage, with its tin enamelled bath and conveniences, well ventilated and drained ; and the gardens, with their little rockeries, bounded by the ugly cast-iron railing, and the pathway of hard stable-brick to the entrance-door. This is the popular idea of the country cottage to-day. The type is almost universal, and its cost, if not its characteristics, is the standard for all others. The " hundred-and-fifty-pounds " cottage is only the " ideal " in another garb. Cheapness, not good building, is its first aim—something pretty at the price, and cheaper if possible.

It is strange and wonderful that an intelligent person should imagine that good work and good building can be obtained without an increased expenditure of time and thought, and that, with such an idea, the new could be possibly as good as the old. Money spent in competitions to achieve the impossible, would be far better laid out in the encouragement of village industries, and in picking up again the local and traditional methods of work. Or it might be used for the education of local authorities in matters which affect the village crafts. They require it ; for of what use can it be for educational bodies like the Art Workers' Guilds, the Arts and Crafts Schools in town or village to increase the number of workers really interested

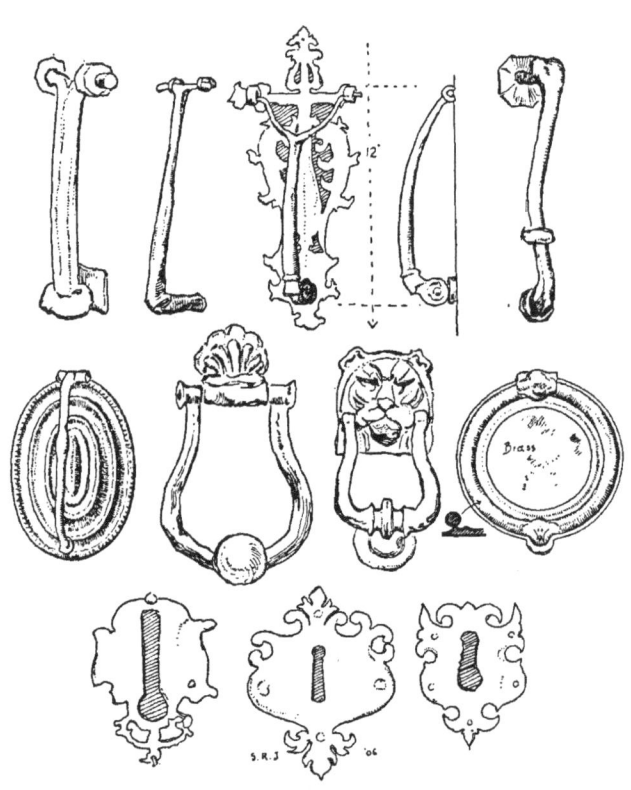

CAST AND WROUGHT IRON DOOR KNOCKERS AND LOCK PLATES

166

in what they attempt to do, if local bodies discourage the use of traditional methods and material. This is one of the most pressing problems of beautiful building, both in the towns and in the agricultural districts. On the one hand there is the gradual increase of interest in the Arts and Crafts Schools, turning out from year to year a number of able craftsmen ; while on the other hand there is the discouragement by local authorities of some of the very trades being taught in the schools. The establishment of more craft schools in the villages, locally controlled, is probably one of the steps towards the revival of country crafts along the old lines, providing there grows up at the same time a more intelligent recognition by the public of the beauty of good work in preference to that which is poor and cheap, and of which we seem to be getting, perhaps, a little ashamed.

That the new cottage, with all its modern appliances, is a dismal failure, there can be no doubt. Quite apart from any sentimental or historical considerations, the old English cottage is altogether more admirable and pleasant to live in than the new. The walls, notwithstanding what has been said of their defects in construction, are generally more satisfactory than 9-in. walls and rough-cast ; the materials are better and used generously. The plan, too, is superior, for it is based on an architectural idea—" the bay " with transepts or aisles, whereas the new is merely an economical and convenient arrangement of rooms without relation to a central idea.

G. Ll. Morris.

Window balcony in Iron
Henley in Arden
Warwick"

Iron Garden Gate.
Binton. Warwickshire.

WROUGHT IRON WORK

Sydney R——
——— 1906.

MILTON BRYANT, BEDFORDSHIRE

168

TO EVERYONE
HIS OWN ORCHESTRA.

WITHOUT the resources of the modern orchestra the hearing of much of the grandest music ever written would have been absolutely denied to the world. Music, the most spiritual of the arts, so long crippled by imperfect mechanism, has now attained full power of instrumental expression. This realisation of music, alike to the composer, the performer, and the auditor, is consummated in the Æolian Orchestrelle.

In appearance this instrument somewhat resembles an upright piano; but whereas the piano is a stringed instrument, the Æolian is of the organ principle. Its notes are produced from pipes, the simple sounds of which are softened and refined by qualifying tubes and special air-chambers. This treatment greatly increases the volume of sound. The tone of the Orchestrelle is unique. With its equipment of stops, faithfully producing the effects of flute and horn, of clarinet and piccolo, of violin and 'cello, all the wood-winds, strings and brasses, it is more than an organ adapted to the requirements and limitations of a private house ; it is the evolution and perfection of a new musical instrument.

There is no music which the Orchestrelle will not produce with a purity, delicacy, and range of tone possessed by no other instrument. It is a complete orchestra, embodying

THE ÆOLIAN ORCHESTRELLE. MODEL Y.

all the resources of a full band of instrumentalists. It can be played directly from the keyboard or by delicate mechanism actuated through the perforations of a music-roll, thus relieving the performer of the technical drudgery of playing the notes and, at the same time, requiring his control of expression and time through the stops. For the Orchestrelle is not an automatic instrument ; it undertakes the production of the notes as the fingers of a pianist are trained to pro-

duce them mechanically. But the brain of the player is no less at work upon the music of the Orchestrelle than it is upon the fingers of the pianist. In each case it is the mind and emotion of the performer that give individuality, colour, and effect to the music. This may be thought impossible, and Madame Melba has confessed to the prejudice. She has also recanted, and written : " When I first heard of the Æolian Orchestrelle, I was unable to understand how a musical instrument requiring no technical knowledge could be artistic from the musician's standpoint. I do not think it possible for anyone to understand it unless they do as I did—see it and hear it played."

The musical value of the Æolian Orchestrelle is immense—incalculable. All music is its province, and perfect rendering its *forte*. It brings all the resources and entertainment of the concert-hall straight into the home. It offers the whole wealth of music to the lover of harmony. For instance, if Brahms be the favoured composer, there is no occasion to sit out four-fifths of a concert to attain the desired fifth. The Æolian renders all Brahms when, where, and as repeatedly as desired. The Æolian does not dictate the *nuances*, tones, variations of rhythm and execution ; it places these in the hands of the player, and he may either regulate the time, expression, and stops according to the markings shown on the roll, or he may vary them according to his own sense of music. The hand-player has drilled his fingers into such certainty and automatism of action that they undertake the executive work for him. The Æolian Orchestrelle undertakes the same work for anyone, so that, in the words of De Reszke, the famous tenor, " If the performer can grasp the inspiration of the composer, the instrument affords him every facility for interpreting the music with feeling." All that gives colour, expression, and individuality to the music is of the player's making. In other words, he has a technically-skilled orchestra entirely subordinate to his own will. Two renderings of any particular orchestral work would no more agree than if they were played manually, for the Æolian is not a mechanical instrument ; it is played with brains.

Famous musicians throughout the world are united in their appreciation of the Æolian Orchestrelle. Pianists like Paderewski, de Pachmann, Hofmann ; singers like Melba, Calvé, and the brothers De Reszke ; violinists like Ysaye and Sarasate; composers like Puccini, Luigi Arditi, and Massenet ; teachers like Sir Alexander Mackenzie, Sir Hubert Parry, and Dr. Turpin — these are musicians whose critical and artistic power no one can question, and they, with many others, hail the Æolian Orchestrelle

The virtuoso appreciates the Æolian Orchestrelle because he, above all, can recognise the wonder of its technique, its marvellous beauty of tone and unique combination of the power and tone-effects of all musical instruments. Moreover, he is aware of its inestimable value in the musical education of the public and in the cultivation of a love of music. No other instrument places the whole of orchestral music within the productive capacity of everyone who has musical taste, whatever his lack of technique.

Paderewski has written that the Æolian Orchestrelle combines " all the effects which can be produced by the most skilful manipulation of a grand organ with those of an orchestra. The execution of even the most com-

plicated passages leaves nothing to be desired ; and what adds to the instrument's value is the magnificent répertoire which, with great care and perfect taste, has been prepared for it. I consider this instrument not only a source of delight to music-lovers, but also a benefit to art itself, as by means of the Æolian the masterpieces, through a thus easily obtained production, will greatly gain in appreciation and popularity."

To the student or amateur, with his imperfect technique, the Æolian

THE ÆOLIAN ORCHESTRELLE. MODEL V.

Orchestrelle, with its faultless rendering of any score, subject to the control, in time, tone, and expression, of its player, affords an intimacy with the works, or any particular work, of any composer that no series of concerts or lectures would afford. The owner of an Æolian, and *no one else*, has always at his command the means of playing and hearing at any time, and as many times and in as many variations of time or expression as he likes, the—for example—Ninth Symphony of Beethoven.

The Æolian Orchestrelle is made in several models at a wide range of prices. More practical information, and a proper realisation of the Æolian's place in music, can be obtained in one visit to the Æolian Hall, at 135 New Bond Street, than can be gleaned from pages of printed matter. The Orchestrelle Company is always pleased to welcome any music-lover who wishes for a practical demonstration, and anyone who cannot make it convenient to call, is invited to write for descriptive Catalogue 20.

ND - #0038 - 070325 - C0 - 229/152/14 - PB - 9781333013899 - Gloss Lamination